Eagles

Masters of the Sky

Rebecca L. Grambo, Editor

An Anthology of Writing, Photography, and
Art from Throughout the World

With selections from Richard R. Olendorff, George Laycock, John James Audubon,
Native American legends and folklore from around the world

RAINCOAST BOOKS

Vancouver

DEDICATION

*To Glen, because you encourage me to try my wings, help keep the wind beneath them,
and are always there when my landing is less than ideal.*

Edited by Jane Billinghurst
Designed by Leslie Ross
Printed in China

97   98   99   00   01   5   4   3   2   1

Canadian Cataloguing in Publication Data
Main entry under title:
Eagles
    Includes bibliographical references and index.
    ISBN 1-55192-098-0
    1. Eagles. 2. Eagles—Pictorial works. I. Grambo, Rebecca, 1963–
QL696.F32E23 1997   598.9'42   C97-910307-X

First published in Canada in 1997 by
Raincoast Books
8680 Cambie Street
Vancouver, B.C. V6P 6M9
(604) 323-7100

First published in the United States in 1997 by Voyageur Press, Inc.
123 North Second Street, P.O. Box 338, Stillwater, MN 55082 U.S.A.

Page one: *An image of grace and power, a bald eagle soars high over its domain.* (Photo © Frank Oberle)
Page two: *A lone bald eagle waits out a snowstorm.* (Photo © Terry Berezan / Wilderness Images)
Page three inset: *Eagle image from the Kwakiutl people of British Columbia.*
Page five: *Golden eagle.* (Photo © Tom & Pat Leeson)

Permissions
We have made every effort to determine original sources and locate copyright holders of the excerpts in this book. Grateful acknowledgment is made to the writers and publishers listed below for permission to reprint material copyrighted or controlled by them. Please bring to our attention any errors of fact, ommission, or copyright, so we may correct them in subsequent editions.
Jeffers, Robinson. *The Collected Poetry of Robinson Jeffers, Vol. 2, 1928–1938.* Tim Hunt, ed. Stanford, CA: Stanford University Press. Copyright © 1938 and renewed 1966 by Donnan Jeffers and Garth Jeffers. Copyright © 1995 by the Board of Trustees of the Leland Stanford Junior University. Reprinted by permission of Stanford University Press.
Laycock, George. *Autumn of the Eagle.* New York: Charles Scribner's Sons, 1973. Copyright © 1973 by George Laycock. Reprinted by permission of Charles Scribner's Sons.
Olendorff, Richard R. *Golden Eagle Country.* New York: Knopf, 1975. Copyright © 1975 by Richard R. Olendorff. Reprinted by permission of Alfred A. Knopf Inc.

Contents

Introduction

I am fortunate enough to have encountered many kinds of animals, from aardvarks to zebras, and from moose to mice. Perhaps it says something about their uniqueness that only with eagles can I recall exactly when I first saw one.

I was driving east across South Dakota, on break from university and headed home for Thanksgiving. It was a typical, blustery gray November day, and I was looking forward to stopping for coffee at Chamberlain on the Missouri River. As I reached the curves that signaled the descent to the river, I saw a big bird floating over the road and on toward the water. It took a moment for the flash of white head and white tail to register, but then—an eagle! I'd seen an eagle! I eagerly scanned the skies and shoreline as I drove on across the river, but there was no further sign of the bird. A fleeting glimpse that made my heart pound and my brain sing, an image so clear that I can recall it now, fifteen years later, with little effort—that's the power of the eagle.

I've seen many more eagles since then and each time I feel that catch of breath, that sense of wonder. I'm not alone—eagles have captured human imagination wherever, and for as long as, the two species have shared a home. Eagles can cause even hardened biologists to allow words like "magnificent," "beautiful," and "incredible" to creep into otherwise scientifi-cally sterile descriptions. Perhaps it's their size or aristocratic gaze, or perhaps it's our awe tinged with envy of the eagle's ability to soar effortlessly above us. Whatever the cause, in myths and legends, as symbols of great power, eagles soar through human history on strong wings.

At some point, however, there was a significant change in the relationship. As people lost frequent contact with wilderness and wild creatures, something was lost, a connection was broken. Eagles, and other animals, became resources to be exploited or vermin to be exterminated. The past two centuries in particular have been a battle for survival for eagles—persecution and pesticides have reduced their numbers, in some cases to the brink of extinction.

This book is an exploration of eagles, their strength and beauty, through the words of ancient legends and the observations of writers past and present. These writings provide important keys to understanding how humans transformed eagles from heroes to villains. The dark hours are not completely behind us, but there is good reason for hope. My wish is that the combination of ancient magic and current facts can reestablish part of the broken connection and help us reach a new appreciation of the value and power of eagles.

FLYING BALD EAGLE
Facing page: *A solitary bald eagle flies ahead of a flock of gulls.* (Photo © Thomas D. Mangelsen)

Above, inset: *Eagle image from the art of Southwestern Native Americans.*

Discovering Eagles

In the beginning there was only water. Overhead an eagle flew, searching for a dry place on which to lay her egg. Far in the distance she glimpsed what appeared to be a piece of solid ground so on she traveled. Exhausted, she finally landed and laid her egg, tucking it gently underneath her feathers as she settled to brood. But the "land" on which she had chosen to nest was actually the knee of the sorcerer Vainamoinen, who lay sleeping in the water below. The heat from the eagle began to burn the sorcerer's knee and he stirred in his sleep, moving his leg restlessly. The eagle egg tumbled into the water and broke. From the yolk of the egg, the moon and the sun were formed; the shattered shell became the firm earth and the sparkling stars.
—Finnish creation myth

To begin our voyage of discovery into the world of eagles, it makes sense to go back in time. How ancient people viewed eagles—and the stories they told about these great birds—gives us a foundation upon which to build. Eagles were greatly respected, and they were credited with extraordinary, sometimes frightening, powers. In some stories, they were given the most powerful role of all—that of Creator.

ANCIENT DESCRIPTIONS

The Kwakiutl Indians of British Columbia tell a story of two eagles who descended from the heavens, and, upon removing their feathers, became a man and a woman. The Tennanai of Alaska say that with the help of a blue jay an eagle created all life. The Buriat people of Siberia believe an eagle is their paternal ancestor, and they place wooden eagles on poles in front of their houses to drive away evil spirits.

BIRD OF LEGEND
Facing page: *Myths and legends about eagles give us insights into the place that eagles held in the world of the past. As noted ornithologist Leslie Brown wrote, "One man's lifetime is not long enough to learn all about eagles."* (Photo © Alissa Crandall)

Above: *Prehistoric Native Americans envisioned this godlike figure that was half human, half eagle. This image appeared on a copper plate found at the Etowah Mound in Georgia.*

BIRD OF PREY

Despite their formidable-looking beaks, the real weaponry of eagles lies in their talons. The basic design is similar for most eagles: three toes directed forward and one backward. Two fish eagle species, the gray-headed fish eagle (Ichthyophaga icthyaetus) and the lesser fish eagle (Ichthyophaga humilis), have two toes pointing each way. The front toes hold the prey, as the back toe punches into it. Specialized modifications have developed for various types of prey: the fish eagles mentioned above have sharp, pointed scales on their toes for gripping slippery fish; snake eagles have short, thick toes that let them hold their squirming prey in a crushing grip. In any case, the grip of an eagle is tremendously strong—something anyone who has been grabbed by one will tell you. (Photo © Lynn M. Stone)

From the Salinan Indians of California comes this creation story, retold from the *Encyclopedia of Creation Myths* (1994):

BACK, FAR BACK in the earliest mists of time, Eagle was magnificent—handsome and very powerful. Sea Woman, who had a great basket holding all the waters of the world, was jealous of Eagle and tried to drown him by pouring out her basket. The water flowed in torrents until only the top of Santa Lucia Mountain remained above the flood. Eagle brought all the animals to this safe haven, and then borrowed Puma's whiskers to make a lasso with which he recaptured the sea basket. Then Sea Woman died, and Eagle asked Dove to fly over the waters and bring back some mud. Eagle took the mud and from it formed a new world. From the wood of the elder bush, Eagle also made a man and a woman. Prairie-Falcon took these new beings to the sweat house and Eagle breathed upon them, giving them life.

Kwakiutl transformation mask
A southern Kwakiutl eagle transformation mask opens to reveal a human face. (Photo courtesy of the Museum of Anthropology, University of British Columbia, Vancouver, Canada. #A4497)

EAGLE EYES

Facing page: *Eagles have remarkable eyesight that is four to eight times better than humans. An object about 1 inch (2.5 cm) long that people could see distinctly at 30 yards (27.5 m) would be clearly visible to an eagle at 120 yards (110 m) and maybe even 200 yards (183 m). While flying along a mountain ridge looking for food, an eagle is able to spot a hare moving about in a valley 2,000 feet (610 m) below. (Photo © Glen & Rebecca Grambo)*

WHITE-TAILED SEA EAGLE

Above: *The white-tailed sea eagle (Haliaeetus albicilla) was extermi-nated in Great Britain in the early 1900s. Reintroduction efforts have lead to the establishment of a small breeding population in western Scotland. However, these eagles are globally threatened by hazardous chemical residues in their food supply as well as by intentional and unintentional poisoning due to predator "control" programs; this bird is pictured in Finland. (Photo © Hannu Hautala)*

Where did these powerful birds come from? There are as many tales about the origins of eagles as there are tellers. Scientists say that the earliest raptors, or birds of prey, lived thirty million to fifty million years ago, and that by about fifteen million years ago, raptors were flying over much of both the Old and New Worlds. These ancient hunters, however, do not appear to be directly linked to our modern raptors, and much of the eagles' evolutionary family tree remains a mystery to ornithologists. Early peoples, however, had no difficulty in describing the origin of the eagles they saw.

The Great-He-She-Spirit, or Manitou, of the Ute Indians created the world and then made all the living things to fill it. From the brightly colored leaves of the forests, Manitou shaped the birds, making the eagles from oak leaves.

The Picuri say that the eagle originally looked something like a crow. Two boys, searching for their parents, met this drab bird, who told them that if they would paint its feathers, it would take them up to the sun. They agreed, coloring the bird's beak and legs yellow and giving it a white tail tipped with black—the colors of a young golden eagle.

As part of their origin myth, the Navahos tell how the war-rior Nayénezgani, after slaying the monster who lived at Winged Rock, turned to the beast's two offspring still in the nest. Left alone, they would have grown up to be evil, but Nayénezgani made them into something beautiful. The younger he turned into an owl, and the elder he made into an eagle, who would furnish his people with feathers for their rites and with bones for their whistles.

The Comanches turn the myth of eagle creating the first people upside down by telling of how, long ago, the young son of a chief died and was turned into the first eagle in answer to his father's prayers to the Creator. The Comanche eagle dance celebrates this legend.

Many other Native American peoples also honor the eagle and seek its power with an eagle dance. Author Gail Tuchman described her experience of the eagle dance in Taos Pueblo, New Mexico, in *Through the Eye of the Feather* (1994). "I re-membered sitting in a firelit circle in Taos witnessing an eagle dance for the first time. The dancer wore a sweeping fan-shaped tail in the back, and attached to his arms from shoulder to fingertips were eagle-feathered wings. With a beautiful, grace-

SHORT-TOED SNAKE EAGLE

Snake eagles, like this short-toed snake eagle (Circaetus gallicus), *often partially swallow their prey head first and then fly to the nest with the tail hanging out of their beak. A young eaglet waiting to be fed will grasp the snake's tail and pull the entire reptile from the parent's crop. One species of fish eagle, the white-bellied sea eagle* (Haliaeetus leucogaster), *is also a snake-eater, plucking sea snakes from the water.* (Photo © Jose Luis Gonzalez Grande/ Bruce Coleman)

AFRICAN TAWNY-EAGLE AND BATELEUR

The same food source may attract more than one diner. Here, in Etosha National Park, Namibia, an African tawny-eagle (Aquila rapax), *left, and a Bateleur* (Terathopius ecaudatus) *tolerate each other long enough to share the remains of a bat-eared fox.* (Photo © Carolyn Chatterton)

IMMATURE BALD EAGLE
Whether caught fresh or eaten as post-spawning carrion, salmon is a bald eagle favorite, as this immature bird shows. (Photo © Lynn M. Stone)

ful flourish of feathers, the dancer began gliding, circling, stomping, soaring, swooping, sweeping from side to side, dipping toward the earth and rising in the air—imitating the movements of the eagle. And in the flurry of feathers and dance, the eagle and the dancer became one spirit."

MODERN DEFINITIONS

*I*f ancient peoples had their own definitions of eagles, today it seems we are not so sure. For scientists, the line between eagle and noneagle is unclear. Eagles belong to the family *Accipitridae*, one of the four groups of raptors, or birds of prey, that make up the order *Falconiformes*.

Although scientists generally agree that eagles evolved from a common ancestor, they don't agree on which birds should be called eagles, sometimes including various hawks, buzzards, and kites. Leslie Brown, a renowned ornithologist who spent his life studying eagles, defined them by exclusion. "An eagle is nowadays best described, rather ambiguously, as a large or very large diurnal raptor which is not a kite, buzzard, vulture, hawk or falcon." In other words, any large predatory bird active mainly by day that does not fall into other, more clearly defined categories is an eagle. By these criteria, there are about sixty species of eagles living around the world, flying over every continent except Antarctica and hunting for prey ranging from sea snakes to dik-diks.

Eagles are loosely divided into four types: sea or fish eagles, serpent or snake eagles, true or booted eagles, and harpy or buteonine eagles. The sea or fish eagles live on the forested shores of oceans, lakes, and rivers from the tropics to the Arctic Circle, except in South America. This group includes the bald eagle (*Haliaeetus leucocephalus*), the white-tailed sea eagle (*Haliaeetus albicilla*), and the vulturine fish eagle (*Gypohierax angolensis*). (Some scientists disagree with this last inclusion, calling the bird the palm-nut vulture and placing it with other Old World vultures.)

The serpent or snake eagles hunt the savannas and forests of tropical Europe, Asia, Australia, and Africa. These are generally smaller eagles, and little is known about many of them. Birds under this heading include the extremely endangered Madagascar serpent eagle (*Eutriorchis astur*) and the flamboyant African bateleur (*Terathopius ecaudatus*).

The true or booted eagles have feathers covering their legs right down to their toes and are found in inland areas throughout the world. This large group includes the golden eagle (*Aquila chrysaetos*), the wedge-tailed eagle (*Aquila audax*), and the hawk-eagles.

The last group, the harpy or buteonine eagles, contains some of the most impressive birds in the world, including the harpy eagle (*Harpia harpyja*), the Philippine eagle (*Pithecophaga jefferyi*), and the crowned eagle (*Harpyhaliaetus coronatus*). (Once again, authorities disagree, some placing the crowned eagle with the sub-buteonine hawks.) These striking eagles, whose habits are not well known, are inhabitants of the tropical forests of South America, Mexico, New Guinea, and the Philippines.

Eagles are as diverse as the terrain over which they soar. The smallest of the eagles, the Nias serpent eagle (*Spilornis cheela asturinus*), has a wingspan of barely 3 feet (1 m), less than many hawks. The largest, the great harpy eagle, has tarsi (the lower parts of its legs) as thick as a child's wrist and a wingspan of over 8 feet (2.4 m). In eagles, females are larger than males, and a female harpy eagle may weigh 15–20 pounds (6.8–9 kg). A bird of prey cannot be much larger than this and still

WEDGE-TAILED EAGLES
This woodcut of a pair of wedge-tailed eagles after a successful hunt appeared in Cassell's Book of Birds *from the 1880s. The artist's choice of prey leaves no doubt about the eagles' home, Australia.*

WEDGE-TAILED EAGLE
For many years, the easiest way to see a wedge-tailed eagle (Aquila audax) in Australia was to look at one of the thousands of carcasses hanging on fences in ranch country. Relentlessly persecuted as a "lamb-killer," this eagle is actually a valuable ally to the rancher, eating rabbits that compete with livestock for forage. (Photo © Gerry Ellis/Ellis Nature Photography)

fly easily. One owner of a female harpy eagle pointed out that the problem didn't so much lie in getting her to fly to his fist, but rather in being adequately braced and padded to survive her arrival!

Depending on the species of eagle and the season, a meal for an eagle may include hare, duck, flamingo, hyrax, salmon, or simply carrion *du jour*. Prey may be as small as termites, which are taken in great quantities when they are swarming, or as big as a young bushbuck, which at 30 pounds (13.6 kg) is too large to be carried off in one piece. Small mammals are mainstays on the menu, but birds, fish, amphibians, and snakes may also make up part or most of an eagle's diet. The unique, near-vegetarian vulturine fish eagle feeds almost exclusively on the fruit of the oil palm, resorting to the occasional small fish, crab, or carrion only when necessary.

Scientists are still working out the relationship between the four groups of eagles, and between eagles and other raptors. Biological and behavioral similarities between sea eagles and kites lead scientists to believe that the sea eagles developed from kites. The snake or serpent eagles seem to be related to the African harrier hawks, but appear to have evolved a form similar to the kites. The harpy eagles appear not to be closely related to any other group, and may be relicts of old lineages. The true or booted eagles are closely related within their group, but, in general, show no strong relationships to other raptors and share just a few similarities with the kites. The formal classification of all raptors, not just eagles, is far from settled, and changes are continually occurring as genetic studies reveal new information.

Ancient peoples were not restricted by modern ideas of species classification, and they added to their list of eagles great birds that soared only in the skies of human imagination. By far, the most well traveled of these fantastic creatures is the Thunderbird.

HARPY EAGLE
Considered to be the most formidable eagle in the world, the magnificent harpy eagle is threatened by deforestation of its home in South America and by direct human persecution. (Photo © Neil Rettig Productions, Inc.)

THE THUNDERBIRD

The Thunderbird, often described simply as a "giant eagle," appears in legends around the world, but it is perhaps best known from the tales of northern people. In the earliest times, the great eaglelike Thunderbird lived in a nearly empty world, among the Dènè people of the icy tundra. Swooping down from the clouds, the great bird flew just above the frigid water, touching it with his wingtips. When he did this, the earth rose from the ocean bottom and floated gently on the water's surface. In northern Asia, when the giant Thunderbird dies, the Upper Being suspends the bird's immortal heart from a thread in the sky. As the heart beats, it makes thunder, and after a while the Thunderbird revives. Up on the delta of the Yukon and Kuskokwim Rivers in Canada lives Tinmiukpuk, a great eagle capable of carrying off reindeer and whales.

Many tales from the Pacific Northwest describe a similar bird. The Nootka people relate that an enormous eagle carries whales high in the air. When the eagle drops its burden, the sound of the whale hitting the water makes thunder. Nearby, the Tsimshian describe Hagwelawremrhskyoek, the Sea-monster Eagle, who causes lightning when he blinks and creates thunder when he flaps his huge wings. The Coast Salish Thunderbird dance includes the igniting of a small charge of gunpowder near the entrance to the ceremonial house, representing the lightning flash of the bird's eyes. Rushton Dorman, in *The Origin of Primitive Superstitions* (1881), wrote that the Delaware Indians believed in a guardian spirit soaring far above them in the form of a great eagle:

SOMETIMES, WHEN WELL pleased with them, he would wheel down into the lower regions, and might be seen circling with wide-spread wings against the white clouds. At such times the seasons were propitious, the corn grew finely, and they had great success in hunting. Sometimes, however, he was angry, and then he vented his rage in the thunder, which was his voice, and the lightning, which was the flashing of his eye.

The ancient Greeks, remembering the eagle's role as the messenger of Zeus, thrower of thunderbolts, buried eagle wings in their vineyards to protect them from lightning. The Norse epic

THUNDERBIRD

When you see a flying eagle today, it is easy to understand the source of Thunderbird legends. Soaring on fabulous wings through stories from long ago, the Thunderbird is a giant eagle, magnified to its great size by human awe and respect. (Photo © Frank Oberle)

Edda describes the giant Hraesvelgr, in the form of an eagle, sitting at heaven's edge. The flapping of his wings causes the winds to blow. The epic Kalevala describes the North Wind as a great, invisible eagle, bringing darkness and storms. In the East, Vishnu rides on the back of Garuda, the storm-cloud bird. From the tales of the Arabian Nights flies the Roc, a fabulous bird strong enough to feed its young on elephants. Attracted by its great egg, Sinbad the Sailor was reckless enough to be snatched up by the Roc and carried to the faraway Valley of Diamonds.

Stand on a prairie coulee and watch a golden eagle soaring out of sight into endless blue and you will know how these fabulous eagles gained their power. The great, mysterious birds of legend are real eagles viewed through a magnifying lens of awe and imagination. But if you are privileged to watch any eagle going about its daily business, you will soon realize that the eagles who share our world today are every bit as miraculous as the most gigantic Roc.

Bald eagle perch
Humans may try to measure the eagle's worth in tourist dollars spent versus salmon eaten, but there is immeasureable value in the pleasure of simply watching an eagle. The poet Robinson Jeffers said it well in "Boats in a Fog": "All the arts lose virtue/Against the essential reality/Of creatures going about their business among the equally/Earnest elements of nature." (Photo © Tom & Pat Leeson)

EAGLES OF THE WORLD

Latin species names from Sibley and Monroe, *Distribution and Taxonomy of Birds of the World* (1990); common names from general usage in literature; status from Collar, Crosby, and Stattersfield, *Birds to Watch 2* (1994).

Sea or Fish Eagles

Haliaeetus leucogaster. White-bellied fish eagle (white-breasted fish eagle).

Haliaeetus sanfordi. Sanford's fish eagle (Solomon fish eagle). Vulnerable.

Haliaeetus vocifer. African fish eagle.

Haliaeetus vociferoides. Madagascar fish eagle. Critical.

Haliaeetus leucoryphus. Pallas's sea eagle (band-tailed sea eagle). Vulnerable.

Haliaeetus albicilla. White-tailed sea eagle (grey/European eagle).

Haliaeetus leucocephalus. Bald eagle (American eagle).

Haliaeetus pelagicus. Steller's sea eagle (white-shouldered sea eagle). Vulnerable.

Ichthyophaga humilis. Lesser fish eagle.

Ichthyophaga ichthyaetus. Grey-headed fish eagle (greater fish eagle).

Gypohierax angolensis. Vulturine fish eagle (palm-nut vulture).

Serpent or Snake Eagles

Circaetus gallicus. Short-toed snake eagle (European snake eagle). Includes *C.g. beaudouini.* Beaudouin's snake eagle.

Circaetus pectoralis. Black-chested snake eagle (black-breasted snake eagle).

Circaetus cinereus. Brown snake eagle.

Circaetus fasciolatus. Fasciated snake eagle (southern banded/east African snake eagle).

Circaetus cinerascens. Banded snake eagle (smaller banded snake eagle).

Terathopius ecaudatus. Bateleur.

Spilornis cheela. S.c. cheela. Crested serpent eagle. *S.c. abbotti.* Simeulue serpent eagle (Simalur serpent eagle). *S.c. asturinus.* Nias serpent eagle. *S.c. sipora.* Mentawai serpent eagle. *S.c. natunensis.* Natuna serpent eagle.

Spilornis minimus. Small serpent eagle. *S.m. klossi.* Nicobar serpent eagle.

Spilornis kinabaluensis. Mountain serpent eagle (Kinabalu serpent eagle).

Spilornis rufipectus. Sulawesi serpent eagle (Celebes serpent eagle).

Spilornis holospilus. Philippine serpent eagle. May be a race of *S. cheela.*

Spilornis elgini. Andaman serpent eagle.

Dryotriorchis spectabilis. Congo serpent eagle (African serpent eagle).

Eutriorchis astur. Madagascar serpent eagle (long-tailed serpent eagle). Critical.

True or Booted Eagles

Aquila pomarina. Lesser spotted eagle.

Aquila clanga. Greater spotted eagle (spotted eagle).

Aquila rapax. African tawny eagle (tawny eagle).

Aquila vindhiana. Eurasian tawny eagle.

Aquila nipalensis. Steppe eagle.

Aquila adalberti. Spanish imperial eagle (Adalbert's eagle). Vulnerable.

Aquila heliaca. Imperial eagle. Vulnerable.

Aquila wahlbergi. Wahlberg's eagle.

Aquila gurneyi. Gurney's eagle.
Aquila chrysaetos. Golden eagle.
Aquila audax. Wedge-tailed eagle.
Aquila verreauxii. Verreaux's eagle (black/African black eagle).
Hieraaetus fasciatus. Bonelli's eagle.
Hieraaetus spilogaster. African hawk-eagle.
Hieraaetus pennatus. Booted eagle.
Hieraaetus morphnoides. Little eagle.
Hieraaetus ayresii. Ayres's hawk-eagle.
Hieraaetus kienerii. Rufous-bellied eagle (chestnut-bellied eagle).
Ictinaetus malayensis. Black eagle (Indian black/Asian black eagle).
Polemaetus bellicosus. Martial eagle.
Spizastur melanoleucus. Black-and-white hawk-eagle.
Lophoaetus occipitalis. Long-crested eagle.
Spizaetus africanus. Cassin's hawk-eagle.
Spizaetus cirrhatus. Includes *S.c. limnaeetus.* Changeable hawk-eagle (marsh hawk-eagle). *S.c. cirrhatus.* Crested hawk-eagle. *S.c. floris.* Sunda hawk-eagle.
Spizaetus nipalensis. Mountain hawk-eagle (Hodgson's/feather-toed hawk-eagle).

ORNATE HAWK EAGLE
Clearly illustrating the concept of "booted" eagles, the group to which it belongs, this ornate hawk-eagle (Spizaetus ornatus) from South America has feathers on its legs right down to the start of its toes. (Photo © Tim Laman/Wildlife Collection)

Spizaetus alboniger. Blyth's hawk-eagle.
Spizaetus bartelsi. Javan hawk-eagle. Endangered.
Spizaetus lanceolatus. Sulawesi hawk-eagle (Celebes hawk-eagle).
Spizaetus philippensis. Philippine hawk-eagle. Vulnerable.
Spizaetus nanus. Wallace's hawk-eagle. Vulnerable.
Spizaetus tyrannus. Black hawk-eagle (tyrant hawk-eagle).
Spizaetus ornatus. Ornate hawk-eagle.
Stephanoaetus coronatus. Crowned hawk-eagle (crowned/African crowned eagle).
Oroaetus. isidori. Black-and-chestnut eagle (Isidor's eagle).

Harpy or Buteonine Eagles
Harpyhaliaetus solitarius. Solitary eagle (black solitary eagle).
Harpyhaliaetus coronatus. Crowned eagle (crowned solitary eagle, solitary eagle). Vulnerable.
Morphnus guianensis. Crested eagle (Guianan crested eagle).
Harpia harpyja. Harpy eagle.
Harpyopsis novaeguineae. New Guinea eagle (New Guinea harpy/Kapul eagle). Vulnerable.
Pithecophaga jefferyi. Philippine eagle (monkey-eating/eagle). Critical.

On Eagle Wings

Above all other birds it is the soaring eagle, with its size and weight, that gives the most abiding impression of power and purpose in the air. It advances solidly like a great ship cleaving the swells and thrusting aside the smaller waves. It sails directly where lesser birds are rocked and tilted by air currents.
—Edwin Way Teale, "Bird of Freedom," *Atlantic Monthly*, 1957

No one watching an eagle hang effortlessly in the sky or rocket downward in a sudden swoop can fail to be impressed. Perched imposingly on a lofty branch, an eagle is noteworthy. On the wing, she is suddenly, unquestionably, the ruler of the lands beneath her.

The wings of most eagles are long and broad, making them efficient for soaring. The tips of the feathers at the ends of the wings, the primaries, are tapered so that when the eagle fully extends its wings, the tips are widely separated. This helps to reduce turbulence as air passes over the end of the wing. Forest-dwelling eagles, like the harpy, have shorter, more rounded wings and longer tails than open-land species, probably to help them maneuver through tight areas filled with leaves and branches. The fish eagles' broad wings and short tails give them the lifting power needed to snatch fish and fowl from the water. In contrast, the long, narrow wings and very short tail of the bateleur make it possible for this eagle to cruise over the African savanna at 40–50 miles per hour (64–80 km/h) for hours at a time.

Combine these wings, some of the strongest in the world, with a lightweight body frame made of hollow, air-filled bones. Then add streamlining and insulation made

HUNTING BALD EAGLE
Facing page: *Legendary American ornithologist John James Audubon was thrilled at the sight of the eagle at work, writing in his famous work,* The Birds of America, *"Now is the time to witness a display of the eagle's powers. He glides through the air like a falling star, and, like a flash of lightning, comes upon the timorous quarry."* (Photo © Frank Oberle)

Above: *Eagle petroglyph from the Native People of the Canadian Pacific Northwest.*

with another lightweight material—feathers. To give you an idea of the relative weights, consider this: bones account for only slightly more than 4 percent of a 14-pound (6.4-kg) bald eagle's weight; the eagle's 7,000 feathers account for about another 9 percent. Eagles are among the most powerful fliers on earth, swooping onto prey with tremendous speed and soaring to great heights with little apparent effort.

RIDING THE WINDS

*E*agles use wind, thermals—rising currents of warm air—and updrafts generated by rough terrain, such as valley edges or mountain slopes, to help them soar with minimum wing-flapping, thereby saving precious energy. Long-distance flights, such as the annual migrations of some species, are accomplished by climbing to great heights in a thermal, then gliding "downhill" to catch the next thermal, where the process is repeated.

Migrating eagles and other raptors using the same technique avoid areas where thermals are scarce, such as open water. This means that migrating flocks are sometimes funneled into narrow land corridors, allowing huge numbers of raptors to be observed in these areas at certain times of the year. At Elat, Israel, near the head of the Gulf of Aquaba, 1.2 million raptors of twenty-eight species were counted during the 1985 spring migration.

This reliance on air currents affects the daily behavior of eagles. The heavier a species is, the more dependent it is on the lift provided by thermals, which are strongest during the warmest part of the day. Heavier eagles, therefore, start hunting later in the morning and stop flying earlier in the afternoon than their lighter relatives. Heavy rain can keep eagles grounded, although eagles living in rainy climates are forced to fly despite the weather in order to hunt. Most raptors, in-

SOARING BALD EAGLE
The widely separated and curved primary feathers at the tips of this bald eagle's wings are the eagle's main flight controls, regulating lift and direction of movement. Its tail feathers act as a rudder and help to stabilize the bird's flight. (Photo © Lynn M. Stone)

cluding eagles, seem to spend more time perching than flying, but, as Richard Olendorff recorded in *Golden Eagle Country* (1975), when they do take wing, we can only stand and wonder:

MARCH 16TH HAD dawned in snow, but by midmorning the sun's rays frequently pierced heavy clouds to accent the beauty of grainfields, leafless trees in creek beds, and gentle east-facing slopes of prairie. Every fence post, tree, and bush was lightly rimed with a sparse stippling of snow.

I watched the perched eagle take flight from the cliff top and begin searching for lifting air currents, while her mate moved out of sight to the south. Air near the ground warmed and rose in large bubbles—called thermals—made visible by the female eagle climbing effortlessly, five hundred, seven hundred, and still many feet higher. She circled masterfully on the thermal's edge with wings as full as a schooner's sails in a steady wind, and my thoughts rode with her.

Her wingspread was nearly seven and a half feet, probably half a foot more than her mate's. The only distinctive feature of her underparts was the contrasting of her dark brown under-wing and body feathers with her lighter brown and slightly barred wing and tail quills. Underneath and from a distance, she appeared simply as a large dark bird. Her wings were bent slightly at the wrists, halfway between her body and the tips. As she wheeled to stay in the thermal, she banked and showed the deep golden hackles of her nape and the equally golden leading edge of each wing. Her wings were wide through most of their length, yet the tips were slotted like an open hand. . . . With sensitive and precise changes of the wing-slot spacing in response to natural air turbulence, she sailed along as fluidly as the air currents themselves.

Thus she soared, changing direction by subtly altering the positions of her wings or, more often, by twisting her tail to catch the wind currents. She trimmed her own sails—skippered herself through the sea of air. At times she slipped smoothly sidewise: by positioning the leading edges of her wings a little to the right of the wind in her face, and tilting her tail down and to the right, the combination of forces pushed her to the right. Occasionally she turned her back to the air currents and sped rapidly windwayward a few hundred yards. When she turned to face her source of lift again, she was circling in a

HARPY EAGLE WITH SLOTH
Ornithologist Leslie Brown wrote that an African fish eagle, swooping for a fish at 20 mph (32 km/h), develops more than 5,000 foot-pounds (6,780 Newton-meters) of energy—that's more than the muzzle energy of a bullet shot from a heavy rifle. A female harpy eagle at the same speed generates 13,500 foot-pounds (18,300 Newton-meters). Imagine being a sloth placidly hanging from a branch when that hits you. This woodcut of a harpy eagle after a successful hunt appeared in Cassell's Book of Birds *from the 1880s.*

BATELEUR
*The colorful bateleur (*Terathopius ecaudatus*) gets its name from a French word meaning "tumbler"—a reference to the sometimes rocking motion of its flight. Like a delta-wing aircraft, the bateleur's wings are angled back toward its body when it flies. Eagles may also spread their wings while on the ground to intimidate intruders, as this bird is doing in the Kalahari Desert of South Africa. Bateleurs are unusual eagles because the males and females have distinctive coloration, making them clearly identifiable at a distance; this is an immature bird.* (Photo © Jeremy Woodhouse)

different thermal. She was fully endowed with beauty, with strength, and with skill; she had a feather for every wind.

Leslie Brown, in *Eagles of the World* (1976), also admired the flight of eagles:

EAGLES OF ALL sorts are seen at their best when soaring; the mastery and control they can then exhibit is superb. Two Scottish Golden Eagles seen under almost completely opposing conditions illustrate this well. The first was soaring below me along the southern face of Ben a Chlachair near Loch Laggan on a day so warm and still that I lit my pipe on the summit without shielding the match. The smoke rose practically without wavering; yet in air so still that neither I nor the smoke of my pipe could detect appreciable currents, the eagle moved easily along from pitch to pitch, the spread primaries at the wingtip gently opening and closing as if delicately fingering the light air currents of that summer's day. His body seemed

29

STELLER'S SEA EAGLE

The magnificent Steller's sea eagle (Haliaeetus pelagicus) *is the third-largest eagle in the world and the largest of the sea eagles—females can weigh over 18 pounds (8.2 kg). Living along the rivers and seacoasts of northeastern Siberia, it winters in Japan and Korea; this bird is pictured on the island of Hokkaido, Japan. Ongoing development in its breeding and wintering areas is threatening this species, which has an estimated breeding population of only 2,200 pairs. (Photo © Orion Service & Trading Co., Inc./Bruce Coleman)*

rock-steady; only his wingtips moved in relation to the plane of flight.

In contrast, on Sgurr na Ciche in West Invernesshire, on a day of hurricane-force wind that tore great slabs of turf off rockfaces and hurled them away like dry leaves, a Golden Eagle soared above a pass, as rock-steady as the bird on Ben a Chlachair, but with his wings three-quarters furled to his sides. He was actually shooting through the airstream at perhaps a hundred air miles per hour, yet appeared to be nailed motion-less against the sky. The eagle on Ben a Chlachair was probably hunting; that on Sgurr na Ciche probably merely playing in the wind. Both gave unforgettable exhibitions of mastery and grace.

THE HUNTING EAGLE

*E*agles seem content to drift when they are looking for prey, but once they spy a likely target, the leisurely aspect of their flight vanishes. Charles G. D. Roberts described it well in *The Lord of the Air* (1904):

THE EAGLE LIFTED and spread the sombre amplitude of his wings, and glided from his perch in a long curve, till he balanced above the unconscious voyager. Then down went his head; his wings shut close, his feathers hardened till he was like a wedge of steel, and down he shot with breathless, appalling speed.

Herbert Ravenal Sass, in *On the Wings of a Bird* (1929), recorded this memorable scene:

THE SHALLOW WATERS of the river flats were packed and crammed with life. From farther South, regiment after regiment of wild ducks had come in: big, burly-bodied mallards, compact, keen-winged teal, slim graceful pintails, already beginning by easy stages their long journey to the far northern breeding grounds. The sunlight, striking downward through the morning mists, glittered on a thousand iridescent green heads, illumined the snowy breasts and necks of the pintail squadrons, lit the white cheek crescents of the blue-winged teal. More numerous even than the ducks, a multitude of coots moved here and there along the reedy margins, their blue-black heads bobbing awkwardly as they swam, their white bills gleaming like polished nickel.

A half mile upstream the river swung to the west in a sharp curve, and there a long, narrow peninsula, densely wooded with tall pines, thrust outward like a lofty promontory halfway across the flats. Suddenly, from behind this promontory, a dark shape sailed into view—a great white-headed eagle, planing on motionless pinions some sixty feet above the surface of the water.

For half a minute nothing happened. Then swiftly the panorama was transformed. The life that crowded the flooded flats, the feathered fleets that had been floating idly there, awoke to instant activity. Near the pine promontory the surface of the lagoon heaved upward, while at the same moment a surging, rushing sound filled the air. Directly in front of the eagle a flock of mallards had risen with a drumming thunder of pinions; and that thunder was a signal to all the vari-coloured multitude thronging that watery world.

Squadron after squadron, regiment after regiment, the wild duck armies lifted from the surface. The air shook with the swelling roar of their wings, with the palpitant clamour of companies of coots scurrying madly across the water. Swiftly the teeming flats were emptying themselves of life. In a tumult of whirring wings and a turmoil of pattering, splashing feet, the legions of the waterfowl were fleeing before their master and sovereign.

I do not know whether the heart of the oncoming eagle swelled with pride and exultation at that moment, but I know that mine always beats faster when I see a sight like the one that I have attempted to describe. . . . Once seen, it will never be forgotten.

TO WIN A MATE

*T*he flight skills of hunting eagles are indeed remarkable. Their most spectacular aerial feats, however, are reserved for each other. The courtship displays of some species of eagles are awesome demonstrations of speed, skill, and power. Richard Olendorff, in *Golden Eagle Country* (1975), wrote of witnessing such a display:

MOST COURTSHIP OF golden eagles is aerial—spectacular dives, mock battles, and other aerobatics. After I had waited for half an hour, the perched eagle left the bank and climbed to more than two thousand feet, in my best estimate. I had to step out of the truck to watch, but that did not seem to change the bird's behavior. It was soon joined by another eagle, presumably its mate. They soared together, mostly over the eyrie, for several minutes. Finally, one bird positioned itself several hundred feet above and upwind of the other. With wings half folded, and with convincing speed and directness, the higher eagle made a swooping approach to its mate. I assumed, thereafter, that the "attacker" was the male. At the last moment, his mate flipped upside down to present open talons in mock combat, but she quickly regained herself and dived several hundred feet. The tiercel [male eagle] passed over her, leveled his path, then quickly climbed a hundred feet, letting the force of the follow-through from the dive carry him upward. But, seeing his mate growing smaller below him, he immediately folded his wings and dropped toward her again, repeating the previ-

COURTSHIP FLIGHT

George Laycock poetically described the courtship flight of eagles in his book, Autumn of the Eagle: *"Up and over they pinwheel down the spring sky until it seems they will crash to earth. But then they break apart and, on heavy wings, lift themselves away to the security of the eagle's sky again."* (Photo © Frank Oberle)

ous false show of aggression. I hated to see him surge by her, because that meant the end of another spectacular stoop; nothing plummets quite like a golden eagle. His third approach was a slow, shallow glide, legs extended downward and yawing from side to side. His mate was moving off to the east as he pulled in six feet behind her. Together, in tandem, they turned northeast. . . . My field notes said only: "Eagle courtship flight!" I will be able to replay that flight in my mind as long as I live.

From Herbert Ravenal Sass, *On the Wings of a Bird* (1929), comes this description of two Bald Eagles in courtship flight:

THOSE FEW MOMENTS were memorable—the great birds dark against the blue . . . heavens, their white heads and tails shining in the bright sun, their mighty sombre wings lashing the air, driving them onward in swift flight or in swifter pursuit, all the passion of their fierce desire blazing there in the face of the sky, each wholly intent upon the other, each heedless of all else in the whole universe except the splendid snowy-headed being that was the one thing worth possessing in all the world.

Perhaps Walt Whitman did these remarkable birds the most justice with his poem, "The Dalliance of Eagles."

Till o'er the river pois'd, the twain yet one, a moment's lull
A motionless still balance in the air, then parting, talons loosing
Upward again on slow-firm pinions slanting, their separate diverse flight
She hers, he his, pursuing.

Skyward in air a sudden muffled sound, the dalliance of the eagles
The rushing amorous contact high in space together
The clinching interlocking claws, a living, fierce, gyrating wheel,
Four beating wings, two beaks, a swirling mass tight grappling,
In tumbling turning clustering loops, straight downward falling,

Born in a Lofty Aerie

The bold eagle, which man's fear enshrouds,
Would, could he lodge it, house upon the clouds.
—John Clare, "Shadows of Taste"

For all eagles, life begins in an aerie, in some cases a place that has seen generations of eagles grow to take their first flight. For adult eagles, the nest is the focal point of their lives and the center of their attentions and energies for a good portion of each year.

THE NEST

Our knowledge about many species of eagles is still limited to the part of their lives that occurs around their nests, as that is often the only place they can be observed with any regularity. Over the years, facts have replaced speculation and our concept of the eagle's home life has changed.

In 1876, Edward Newman, in "The Eagles of Poetry and Prose," *The Zoologist,* described a fantasy version of the eagle's nest:

[THE EAGLE'S] EYRIE is a palace, where he feeds sumptuously every day, he and his spouse and the little ones. Woe to the cragsman who attempts to reach that eyrie! it

BALD EAGLES GUARDING NEST
Facing page: *Eagles living in the temperate zone nest early, giving their chicks enough time to grow, fledge, and learn to hunt before approaching winter drives them south. Unfortunately, that sometimes means putting up with the occasional late spring snowstorm.*
(Photo © Alan & Sandy Carey)

Above: *Eagle image from a Zuñi shield from the southwestern United States.*

would be certain death: it were safer to beard the lion in his den than to approach the monarch of the air in his exalted eyrie: cutlass and blunderbuss would prove unavailing: from the moment the cragsman makes the attempt his fate is sealed. Such is the eagle of poetry, the eagle of the imagination!

In 1973, George Laycock, in *Autumn of the Eagle*, gave a more realistic description of the aerie:

THE EAGLE SOARING against the sky seems free. As free as the clouds, the winds, the fog drifting across the lake. Yet, in reality, the eagle is not free at all, except perhaps when young and not yet anchored to mate or eyrie.

For the rest of its life, if it succeeds in entering the breeding population, the eagle lives in bondage, not to the mate, but to the master of both, the territory and particularly the giant treetop nest to which it has become a lifelong caretaker. Wherever the eagle travels, its home territory exerts a magnetic force drawing it back. The eagle's freedoms become little freedoms. It may choose the perch on which it rests, the food it pursues, the hour when it hunts, but it does not escape the demands of the eyrie. The choice is not its own.

The life of the eyrie may span the decades. If an eagle's mate dies, the survivor, still tied to the home territory, is driven to travel beyond the distant hills, rivers, and lakes, searching for a new mate.

The old nest becomes, in turn, master of the latest arrival. Then if its mate should die, it may in turn depart in search of a mate and, with good fortune, bring another strange eagle to share the nest which neither of them built but both will repair, maintain, and use as long as they or the nest remain. In this way the eagle's nest spans the generations.

BALD EAGLE NEST
The large nest of the bald eagle pair, showing a classic wine-glass shape, will be both nursery and gymnasium for their offspring. Often undergoing additions for many years, the nests can become huge structures if the underlying supports are strong enough. Although bald eagles prefer to nest in trees, in the tree-barren Aleutian Islands a nest may consist of only a seaweed mound on the ground. (Photo © W. Perry Conway)

BONELLI'S EAGLE

This Bonelli's eagle (Hieraaetus fasciatus) *is winging its way nestward with a fresh spray of greenery. Eagles often bring green branches to the nest during the courtship and early chick-rearing period, but the reasons for this behavior are still unknown.* (Photo © Antonio Manzanares/ Bruce Coleman)

Once it reaches sexual maturity, at around four to five years of age, an eagle's energies become concentrated on the effort of finding a mate and raising its offspring. The all-important nest may be built in a tree, on a cliff, or even on the ground if there are no other options available. Some eagles, like the brown snake eagle, make small, poorly constructed nests every year. The bateleur builds a larger, more solid structure and uses it for several breeding cycles. The big eagles, like the bald and the golden, build huge nests, sometimes having more than one and alternating use on an annual basis. The big eagles return to their nests year after year, adding fresh material each season. If the underlying support is strong enough, these nests can reach immense proportions. A famous bald eagle nest at Vermilion, Ohio, was 12 feet (3.6 m) tall, 8½ feet (2.6 m) across the top, and weighed an estimated 2 tons (1.8 t)—more than 400 times the weight of one of its builders!

Eagles add sticks and dead branches to their nests by plucking them from the ground or knocking them off trees by flying at the tree and striking the desired branch with their talons. Grass, moss, and other plant material may be worked into any gaps left between the branches. African fish eagles like to use the nests of weaverbirds for gap filling, and also for nest lining. More exotic building materials have also been noted, including whole cornstalks, sometimes with ears still attached, and a 25-foot (7.6 m) length of rope. In 1882, a strange-looking eagle's nest in North Dakota was found, on closer examination, to have been built with buffalo rib bones.

Myrtle Broley, in *Eagle Man* (1952), records that her husband, retired Canadian bank manager and pioneering bald eagle–bander Charles Broley, found his share of unusual objects in Florida nests:

He found a [bleach] bottle, empty of course, and a snap clothes-pin in one eyrie, and wondered if a laundry was contemplated or if the adults had gotten sick of the fishy smell. Another eyrie held a long white candle, broken a bit. Then he found an electric light bulb—a thousand lumen, the type used in street lighting.

Old shoes, gunny or crocus sacks, ears of corn, even a family-group photograph in a heavy frame, were discovered in nests besides, naturally, the remains of animals, fish, and reptiles which the young birds or their parents had devoured. Large shells are common up in Florida eyries, conchs turning up in almost every one. . . .

When there was so much talk a few years ago about the "New Look" for women, Broley saw an eagle flying in to its nest with a long skirt trailing behind. He wondered then if they had become style conscious also. This was not the only ladies' garment found away up in the treetops. A pair of lace-trimmed pink panties reposed coyly in a corner of one big nest. . . .

Up in an eyrie he found a copy of the *American Weekly*, the Sunday supplement for so many papers. Oddly enough, it was opened at an article about the Doukabors [*sic*] in Canada and the trouble they were causing the government of that country by their nude parades. He thought it was exceedingly strange to think that he, a Canadian, should be sitting up in an eyrie in Florida with a half-grown eagle on each side of him, reading this article about far-off Canada.

Aside from all the above, eagles frequently bring sprays of fresh green material to their nests throughout the time they occupy them. More is brought before incubation begins, and the supply begins to taper off as the young birds grow. There have been various theories advanced for this, none of them completely satisfactory. Some speculate that the greens assist the eagles in keeping the nest clean by relining the nest cup and helping to avoid parasite infestations; that they shade the young eaglets; or that they are used by the eagles to decorate the nest. Whatever the reason, a green branch seems to be an exciting possession for eagles. The male brings many to the female while courting her, and often branches are brought when it's time for a shift change while incubating.

The act of constructing or refurbishing a nest seems to bring an urgency to the eagles' daily routine. Although for most eagles copulation occurs throughout their breeding season, mating becomes more frequent during the nest-building period: An amorous pair of African fish eagles was observed mating six times during one morning. Other courtship behaviors also seem tied to the nest. The male banded snake eagle often brings a tasty frog or snake to a favorite feeding place near the nest. There he calls to the female, who flies to him and eats his offering. This may happen almost daily throughout their courtship, and once they have bonded, little deters them from their purpose; banded snake eagles have been observed mating on the ground after tumbling, claws interlocked, from their nest tree.

The time eagles spend working on their nest can be anywhere from a week—for a simple refurbishing job in the temperate zone—to several months, for a new nest in warmer latitudes. Leslie Brown theorized that in colder climates, the birds simply don't have the leisure to move slowly if they are to raise young that are ready to fly when winter comes. Once the nest is considered up to exacting parental specifications, it's not long before the first egg is laid.

From Humble Beginnings

Unremarkable to look at—usually a simple speckled off-white or buff color—the one to three eggs in an eagle's nest represent a great commitment of time and energy by the parents. In most eagle species, the forty-plus days of incubation duty are patiently shared by both the male and the female. During the course of his fieldwork, Richard Olendorff had the following encounter, described in *Golden Eagle Country* (1975):

I LAY DOWN in full view of the incubating female and stared—fifteen-power spotting scope versus supposedly eight-power eyes—into the great depth of an eagle's personality. It was hopeless for me to duplicate her stillness; fifteen minutes or an hour, no matter, an eagle will lie over its eggs without moving a feather.

There was something hypnotic about lying on the ground gazing into the deep brown of that eagle's eyes; it was almost a spiritual experience. The threat of my presence was reflected in the uneasiness of her expression, a look of challenged superiority looming from the advantage of her high nest. Her golden hackles and neck feathers framed the dark sides of her head in striking contrast.

Why would anyone want to destroy such a majestic creature as a golden eagle? I thought. I daresay that guns would be silenced and poisons never strewn over the land if the misinformed could experience a half-hour face-to-face meeting with an incubating eagle.

Once the eggs begin to hatch, the female's vigilance becomes nearly constant. The male assumes the heavy responsibility of providing the majority of the food needed by his rapidly growing family. The female will gradually take up her share of the hunting as the eaglets grow, but in the early days, her attention is fixed on the eaglets tucked beneath her.

Newly hatched, eaglets are a far cry from the strong, fierce creatures they will become: soft, grayish-white down covers their small bodies, their wobbly legs are too weak to hold their weight, and their vision is limited by partially closed eyes. The only protection they have comes from their ever-attentive parents.

The sight of the great female gently coaxing her tiny chick to take a shred of meat from her fiercely hooked beak is one that has mesmerized many observers. She will offer food again and again, eating rejected morsels herself, and then tearing off another piece to present to the eaglet. The adult eagles also seem to take great care not to step on their eggs or chicks when they settle to brood, clenching their great talons into harmless

balls and placing them deliberately so as not to risk accidentally injuring their offspring.

My first trip to a golden eagle's nest, in the company of an authorized eagle bander, was full of surprises. First of all, I dislike heights and stepping backward into space, suspended only by a suspiciously thin rope, is not something I would ordinarily consider doing. However, the prospect of seeing an eaglet made me take that initial step. Despite lots of calming encouragement, my heart was pounding by the time we reached the nest. I immediately forgot most of my fear with my first look at the inhabitants.

I guess I had expected something more imposing than the fluffy white creatures flopping around in the nest and gaping at us. They seemed small and fragile in the large flattened cup of the nest, utterly uneaglelike—until you took a close look at their faces and feet. Their eyes and beaks had a decidedly aquiline cast, hinting at regal profiles to come. And those big, strong talons, so capable of inflicting injury on the unwary bander, left no doubt about the heritage of these babies.

As I became more comfortable in my nest-side perch, I was able to look around at the remnants of the eaglets' meals: here the hind leg of a jackrabbit, over there a mallard wing, some miscellaneous feathers and bones. Over everything hung a rather ripe aroma and a small shifting cloud of flies. As I looked out over the nest edge, I could see the stream of "whitewash" where the eaglets had tidily defecated over the side.

There was no sign of the parent birds, the female having left the nest as we readied for our descent. This is normal for most eagles; they don't viciously defend their young. Instead, heeding their instinct for self-preservation they usually take flight well before an intruder reaches the nest,. Banders will not approach a golden eagle nest in rainy weather, as that would leave the chicks exposed to the elements, and they always keep their visits as short as possible to minimize the time that the female is kept from the nest. Eagles, in general, take great care of their young, doing their best to ensure the survival of the initially fragile chicks. Frances Hobart Herrick, who made one of the first in-depth studies of bald eagles at their nest, recorded the following observations in "Daily Life of the American Eagle," published in *The Auk* in 1932:

TREETOP AERIE
This bald eagle nest will serve as both nursery and gymnasium for the rapidly growing eaglets. Cared for by attentive parents, the chicks will soon be hopping and testing their wings, and be ready to take their first flight about seventy-five days after hatching. (Photo © Michael H. Francis)

WEDGE-TAILED EAGLE NESTLING
This newly hatched wedge-tailed eagle doesn't look much like its parents but time will change that. Eagles lay their eggs over a period of time rather than all at once, so this fuzzy nestling will probably soon have a sibling to sharing its home and food. (Photo © Lloyd Nielsen/Oxford Scientific Films)

GOLDEN EAGLE NESTLING
Staring at the strange intruders that have come to its nest, this still-downy golden eagle nestles among the pungent remains of many meals. Its sibling, still too wobbly to hold its head up for long, rests alongside. (Photo © Glen & Rebecca Grambo)

SHE STOOD FACING the wind and rain, with half-open wings, and afforded good shelter for the month-old eaglets huddled beneath her. In a few minutes this shower passed, and as the sun broke out she went back to her perching tree and spread her drooping wings to dry. . . . Now, a quarter of an hour had hardly passed before the clouds again closed in and darkened above us; another downpour was under way, and the faithful mother sped back to her charges, and there she remained fending them with her stalwart body until this final shower was over. . . .

[On another occasion,] the male eagle, after having fed his young for twenty minutes in the course of the afternoon, began to dig into the nest from time to time, taking mouthfuls of earth and shifting them to other places, as if bent on smoothing out the inequalities of their bed, and arranging everything to accord with his taste. Occasionally he would pause to look over his eaglets who lay stretched before him.

CAIN AND ABEL

Eagles lay their eggs several days apart, rather than all at once. This means that the chicks hatch one at a time and that the firstborn usually has a size advantage over later arrivals. In some eagle species, this advantage is used by the eldest to kill any nestmates in what has become known as "Cain and Abel" behavior, or simply "Cainism." Respected naturalist and writer Seton Gordon—quoted in Arthur Cleveland Bent's *Life Histories of North American Birds of Prey* (1937)—described the behavior clearly:

TWENTY MINUTES AFTER the parent had left the family, Cain commenced a very determined and entirely unprovoked attack upon her brother. She tore from his unfortunate person great billfuls of white down and even tiny feathers. Abel in desperation ran to the far side of the eyrie and lay there, quite still and very sullen. Cain thereupon stood up, flapped her downy wings, and uttered several wild and piercing yells of victory. There was an extraordinary and quite unearthly quality in these calls which deeply impressed itself upon my mind. Great billfuls of her brother's down adhered to her bill, and

she had much trouble in ridding herself of the fruits of her easily gained victory.

Eventually, the smaller chick dies and is usually consumed by either the survivor or its parents. For the eagles, the eaglet's corpse is nothing more than food that should not be allowed to go to waste.

Scientists have observed Cainism in several species of eagles, but are still unsure of the reasons behind it. It doesn't seem to be merely fighting for food, as Cainism may occur even when there is ample food at the nest. From her studies of Verreaux's eagles, Valerie Gargett noted that the younger chick would just as readily kill the elder were it physically able, and believes that it is genetically determined that a chick will kill its sibling. She goes on to say that she believes that this behavior may have evolved at a time when it was in some way advantageous, and still exists because it's not a detriment to species' survival.

But for some eagles, like the lesser spotted eagle, Cain and Abel behavior has become a problem, given the declining numbers of the species. Scientists have successfully removed eaglets in this situation from the nest and fostered them under other birds, saving these needed additions to the population from unnecessary death.

FIRST FLIGHTS

Time passes, down is gradually replaced by feathers, and the eaglets grow still stronger. Finally, an important moment arrives. In *An Eagle to the Sky* (1970), Frances Hamerstrom, who spent many hours observing eagles, described the process for one young bird:

THE . . . EAGLET WAS now alone in the nest.

Each time a parent came flying in toward the nest he called for food eagerly; but over and over again, it came with empty feet, and the eaglet grew thinner. He pulled meat scraps from the old dried-up carcasses lying around the nest. He watched a sluggish carrion beetle, picked it up gingerly, and ate it. His first kill.

Days passed, and as he lost body fat he became quicker in his movements and paddled ever more lightly when the wind blew, scarcely touching the nest edge; from time to time he was airborne for a moment or two.

Parents often flew past and sometimes fed him. Beating his wings and teetering on the edge of the nest, he screamed for food whenever one flew by. And a parent often flew past just out of reach, carrying delectable meals: a half-grown jackrabbit or a plump rat raided from a dump. Although he was hungry almost all the time, he was becoming more playful as he lost his baby fat; sometimes, when no parent bird was in sight, he pounced ferociously on a scrap of prairie dog skin or on odd bits of dried bone.

The male eaglet stayed by himself for the most part. He was no longer brooded at night. Hunger and the cold mountain nights were having their effect, not only on his body but on his disposition. A late frost hit the valley, and a night wind ruffled his feathers and chilled his body. When the sunlight reached the eyrie's edge, he sought its warmth; and soon, again, he was bounding in the wind, now light and firm-muscled.

A parent flew by, downwind, dangling a young marmot in its feet. The eaglet almost lost his balance in his eagerness for food. Then the parent swung by again, closer, upwind, and riding the updraft by the eyrie, as though daring him to fly. Lifted light by the wind, he was airborne, flying—or more gliding—for the first time in his life. He sailed across the valley to make a scrambling, almost tumbling landing on a bare knoll. As he turned to get his bearings the parent dropped the young marmot nearby. Half running, half flying he pounced on it, mantled, and ate his fill.

Jon Gerrard and Gary Bortolotti, who wrote about their studies of eagles nesting at Besnard Lake, Saskatchewan, in *The Bald Eagle* (1988), point out that first flights are not always such a smooth and successful operation:

AN EAGLET ON its first few flights will sometimes try to land with the wind behind it. Several times I have seen a fledgling grasp momentarily at its intended perch before realizing that its forward momentum was too great to land successfully. Sometimes the bird manages to continue on its broken flight. Some-times it is slowed enough by grasping at the branch that it falls; tumbling, the young eagle may manage to grasp a lower limb and hold on to perch there. Often the bird ends up on the ground. A particularly tenacious bird may succeed in grasping the branch, but unable to stop, it swings forward and comes to rest hanging upside down, wings extended and drooping, looking like a disjointed, overgrown bat.

Eventually, flying becomes familiar and natural to the young birds. The time from hatching to first flight may be anywhere from 60 days in temperate-zone eagles like the golden eagle and short-toed snake eagle to almost 150 days for the massive harpy. During this time, eaglets are at risk from nest predators, starvation, and, in many cases, their siblings. Thus, that first flight, that first experience of truly being an eagle aloft, is a moment of great triumph.

The young eagles remain in the vicinity of the nest for some time, sharing in the food caught by their parents and honing their own hunting skills. Eventually, they will leave to find a territory of their own. Only the fortunate minority that escape the many hazards that await them, will survive to seek out a mate and begin anew the cycle of the aerie.

TESTING ITS WINGS
Great wings spread wide to embrace the wind, a young bald eagle learns to master the intricacies of flight. (Photo © Frank Oberle)

Golden Eagle

We forgot the flowers and all the other loveliness that clings near to the earth. Out there in the space among the encircling peaks was a great bird, moving slowly on massive outstretched wings, which barely wavered as they felt the air currents that kept the bird aloft. On an easy glide, with perfect control and composure and, it seemed, with inexorable purpose, the [golden] eagle floated into our canyon. For a long time it appeared to hang there above us, but it must have been only a few moments before it slanted on a long downward course and settled into the vegetation on the opposite slope, where it was lost from our view. It was only a brief incident, but there was in it the significance of man's poetic thought of the eagle from ancient times, and I knew that these were better mountains because the eagle was there.
—Olaus Murie, "A Price on His Golden Head," *Audubon Magazine*, 1952

GOLDEN EAGLE
Facing page: In Johnson's Natural History from 1894, S. G. Goodrich and A. Winchell described golden eagles: "Their fire-darting eyes, lowering brows, flat foreheads, restless disposition, and terrific plaints, together with their powerful natural weapons, seem to assimilate them to the tiger rather than the timorous bird."
(Photo © W. Perry Conway)

Above: Man-eagle image from Pueblo pottery from the southwestern United States.

The golden eagle recognizes no arbitrary human boundaries in its flight. Like other birds, it is a "global ambassador," a treasure shared by all those beneath its wings, with ancient ties to the beliefs of many races. It is a soaring symbol of the few wild, open places still remaining in our crowded world.

Probably the most widespread eagle of its size, the magnificent golden eagle (*Aquila chrysaetos*) lives throughout much of the northern hemisphere. It is found in mountainous areas, prairie coulees, and other places where rugged terrain creates abundant updrafts. Soaring on 7-foot (2.1-m) wings, golden eagles are masters of the wind, controlling their flight with the merest movements of wingtip feathers. In the 1830s, John James Audubon wrote in *The Birds of America*:

AUDUBON IMAGE OF THE GOLDEN EAGLE
In his legendary work from the 1830s, The Birds of America, *artist John James Audubon illustrated the golden eagle in a dramatic pose after snatching up its prey.*

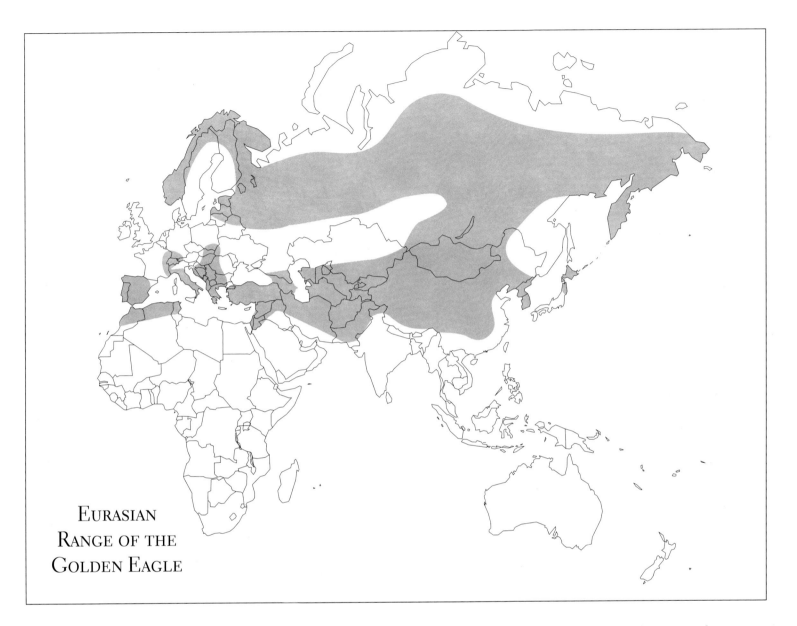

EURASIAN
RANGE OF THE
GOLDEN EAGLE

ALTHOUGH POSSESSED OF a powerful flight it has not the speed of many Hawks, nor even of the White-headed Eagle. It cannot, like the latter, pursue and seize on the wing the prey it longs for, but is obliged to glide down through the air for a certain height to insure the success of its enterprise. The keenness of its eye, however, makes up for this defect, and enables it to spy, at a great distance, the objects on which its preys; and it seldom misses its aim, as it falls with the swiftness of a meteor towards the spot on which they are concealed. When at a great height in the air, its gyrations are uncommonly beauti-ful, being slow and of wide circuit, and becoming the majesty of the king of birds. It often continues them for hours at a time, with apparently the greatest ease.

At times, several eagles may be seen flying together, as Seton Gordon recorded in his observations of golden eagles on the Isle of Skye in *The Golden Eagle* (1955):

ON THAT DAY snow covered the ground. Deep and powdery, it hid each peaty pool and each hill stream. To the east, high cliffs, dark as night, rose against a sky which each moment became more sombre and threatening. The white shroud of the moor and the unrelieved blackness of the precipice formed a fitting picture for what followed. Lifeless and stern was the view until a golden eagle appeared, moving majestically downwind on rigid wings. She—for it was apparent from the great wing-spread that it was a female—swept grandly across a hill pass, and on the far side of the pass, above a flat-topped hill, met three more golden eagles. Those three eagles were almost at once joined by a fifth bird, when an impressive aerial display was begun, which for sheer majesty of flight could not have been excelled. The five eagles, poised at a height of perhaps 1,500 feet above the hill-top, arranged themselves in flying formation and moved majestically against the wind. Higher and higher they mounted on motionless wings, until they entered a cloud layer and were awhile hidden, before descending slightly and reappearing beneath the cloud.

After a time one of the eagles began a series of breathtaking dives. Closing its wings, it fell headlong perhaps 500 feet. It then flattened out, and almost at once mounted until it had regained its lost height, the wings being driven fast and determinedly. As it prepared for the next dive the most spectacular part of the aerial display took place. The eagle's wings still drove it upwards, but the bird slowly tilted, as a rocket does at the end of its climb before falling to earth. The eagle at first fell slowly but when it had got its head down the velocity of the fall at once increased. But even before the flier began to fall the great wings were closed and the angle of the descent was controlled by the tail.

As dusk was approaching the two parties of golden eagles separated and made off in different directions towards their roosting places.

AT HOME IN ROUGH LANDS

Golden eagles usually mate for the first time at the age of four years, and often stay paired with the same mate for their entire fifteen- to twenty-year lifespan. In keeping with their love of wild country, golden eagles prefer to nest on rocky crags or sheer cliff faces, although they will occasionally build a nest in a tree. A mated pair may return to the same nest year

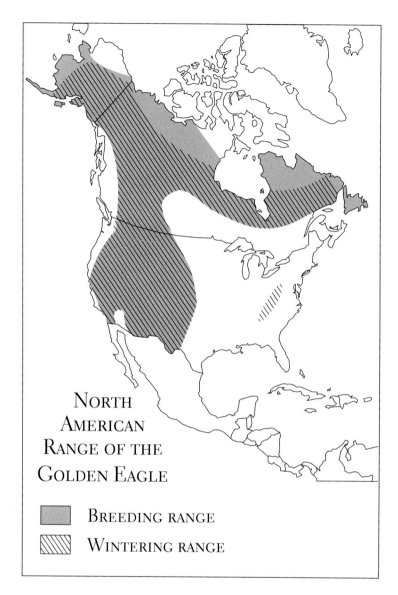

NORTH
AMERICAN
RANGE OF THE
GOLDEN EAGLE

BREEDING RANGE

WINTERING RANGE

GOLDEN EAGLET
Indisputably regal, this young golden eagle looks straight down its beak at the human impudent enough to invade its space.
(Photo © Michael H. Francis)

after year, adding a few inches of new material to the nest top each season. Robert Murphy's description of one nest and its young inhabitants (*The Golden Eagle*, 1965) gives a vivid picture of the eagles' home:

FROM THE ROCKY bank of the small, swift stream at the bottom of the canyon the cliff rose up, straight as a wall, for nearly seven hundred feet into the sky. It was almost a quarter of a mile across its face, sheer and unscalable, as though a great knife had sliced a piece of the mountain away. At each side of the cliff face, framing it, the mountain rose by steep slopes and great rocky steps, by small benches where pines had taken root and clung through storms and winds and the prying fingers of winter ice. About sixty feet below the rimrock at the top, almost equidistant from the sides of the cliff, there was a shelf that thrust out over the empty air for ten feet and ran along the face for twenty. Near one end of it there was a cave four feet wide and six deep; a man on his knees could just about move around in it, and from this cave and the shelf, there was a wide and magnificent view of the canyon, across it over the lower ridge on the other side, and beyond to the far sage brush–dotted Colorado plain that faded off into the haze to the east.

In the middle of the shelf there was a golden eagle's nest made of interlaced sticks and brush and covered on the outside with gray-green moss that blended it into the gray rock of the cliff face. It was small for an eagle's nest, being a little over three feet in diameter and not over two feet high, but this was its first year of occupancy. If the old birds survived the hazards of life, to use it again they would add to it with each succeeding year. It had been dressed around the rim with short pine branches, replaced as they dried and faded, until a week or so past; there were hindquarters of rabbits and several ground squirrels scattered on the shelf near the nest, for the old birds had ceased to remove the remains of prey now that the young were old enough to tear up their own meat.

GOLDEN EAGLE LANDING
Talons outstretched, a golden eagle comes in to its perch. (Photo © W. Perry Conway)

GOLDEN EAGLE IN FLIGHT
The golden eagle prefers the rough land of mountains, coulees, deep valleys, and steep slopes. Here the winds form updrafts on which this magnificent bird soars with unparalleled grace and beauty. (Photo © Alan & Sandy Carey)

There were two young eagles in the nest, one much larger than the other. This was the female, and the earliest hatched; she would always be a third larger than her brother, after the manner of birds of prey. They were both well-feathered, their quills had hardened, and they were about ready to fly; the white natal down that had patched them and tipped their feathers was about gone now, and the clove brown of their plumage had a running purplish sheen. The crown and hackle feathers on the male's head were dark and would grow paler as he matured; the female's were already dark gold and gleamed in the sun. Beneath their wings, at the bases of their primaries, were white patches that would gradually darken. Their tails, except for the dark bands tipped with white at the ends, were white, black-spotted, and would gradually darken too. It would be easy to mistake them now for immature bald eagles at a distance, but their legs were feathered to the toes and the bald eagle's were not.

DANGERS

Golden eagles usually raise one or two young each year (sometimes losing one to Cain and Abel rivalry), feeding them well on a varied diet of which the mainstay is often rabbit or hare. Their preference for prey other than fish helped golden eagles to

GOLDEN EAGLE AERIE
From their nest on the side of a Saskatchewan coulee, these young golden eagles can look out on their future kingdom. Small and fragile now, in only a few weeks these eaglets will make their first tentative flight and, soon after, ride the almost unceasing prairie winds with confidence. (Photo © Glen & Rebecca Grambo)

largely escape the plague of DDT contamination, since the small grass-eating mammals they usually eat are too far down the food chain to have accumulated much pesticide residue. However, their fondness for feeding on carrion has made golden eagles vulnerable to poison from baits set out to kill coyotes and other "pest" species. In addition, deliberate poisoning, shooting, and trapping of golden eagles continues today in all parts of their range, despite laws protecting them. The motivations behind this may be a misguided attempt to protect livestock or an intentional effort to obtain feathers for sale on the black market. Whatever the reason, each eagle killed means fewer chances to see sights like this one described by Seton Gordon in *The Golden Eagle* (1955):

THERE ARE TIMES when the sun is seen to shine on the gold feathers of the eagle's head with beautiful effect. One evening the sun had already set in the glen when an eagle rose from its perch and sailed in spirals, higher and higher. At last the bird reached the rays of the setting sun and its golden head became afire as it caught the sunset light. At the actual moment of sunset the eagle was transformed into a radiant bird, each wing primary being bathed in a pink glow.

FOUNDER OF CITIES

To ancient peoples, the sight of a golden eagle could be a strong omen—strong enough to dictate where a new city would be built. History records that an eagle was responsible for the location of the capital of the Eastern Empire of Constantine. While engineers were surveying the plan of the city at Troy (the emperor's original choice), an eagle swooped down on the measuring line and carried it off, finally dropping it at Byzantium (later Constantinople, now Istanbul). So strong an indication of the gods' intent could not be ignored, and the capital was relocated.

Another legend tells how the forefathers of the Aztec people wandered in search of a suitable location for a city until they saw a sight that settled the matter. Perched on a cactus was a huge eagle, wings outstretched to catch the morning sun and a snake clutched in its talons. The *Crónica Mexicayotl*, written in 1609, gives this version of the event:

In the middle of the water where the cactus stands,
where the eagle raises itself up,
where the eagle screeches,
where the eagle spreads his wings,
where the eagle feeds,
where the serpent is torn apart,
where the fish fly,
where the blue waters and yellow waters join,
where the water blazes up,
where feathers came to be known,
among the rushes, among the reeds where the battle is
*   joined,*
where the peoples from the four directions are awaited,
*   there they*
arrived, there they settled. . . .

—translation by Thelma D. Sullivan

The land that was chosen was near a lake and so swampy that the Aztecs had to sink piles into the soft earth to build their city. Tenochtitlan, which owes its existence to an eagle, is now known as Mexico City.

HUNTING GOLDEN EAGLE
This is the stereotypical golden eagle, rabbit clutched in its talons. Numerous studies have shown that, despite the traditional view of ranchers, live lambs play a negligible role in the diet of most golden eagles. The eagles' undeservedly bad reputation probably originated from observations of them scavenging carcasses. (Photo © Jeff Foott)

Bald Eagle

White-headed and austere on a solitary tree, or flapping and sailing, stiff-winged and spread-fingered, over southern waterways or northern river deltas, inland river swamps or outer beaches, coursing the nation in summer and winter from the Columbia to the Merrimack, from the Everglades to the Yukon, the bald eagle is magnificent.
—Peter Matthiessen, *Wildlife in America*, 1959

The image of the bald eagle (*Haliaeetus leucocephalus*) is one of the most powerful visual symbols in the world today. Chosen to represent the loftiest ideals of America's founding fathers, the bald eagle can be seen in its official form on U.S. coins and currency, on the U.S. Presidential Seal, and on various military medals and insignia of the American armed forces. In less formal incarnations, bald eagles appear around the world in company logos and advertising layouts, in jewelry and clothing designs, and on countless nature-related souvenir items. In its own world, distant from all the glory and hype, the real bald eagle is far more impressive than any of its iconized replicas. Edwin Way Teale, in a 1957 article for *Atlantic Monthly* entitled "Bird of Freedom," shared his impressions:

CLINGING TO SOME lofty perch, it habitually sits erect, its white head of impressive size held high, its yellow eyes surveying with that piercing, concentrated gaze peculiar to its kind the scene spread out below. In every line it imparts an impression of majesty, of unflinching independence. And this is the eagle quiescent.

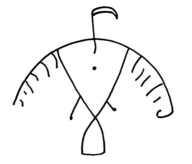

CALLING BALD EAGLE
Facing page: The voice of a bald eagle ringing out over a northern lake is, for many North Americans, as much a symbol of the wilderness as the cry of the loon. Not known for beautiful songs, eagles are most vocal when declaring their territories or calling their mates. Heard frequently around the lakes and rivers where it lives, the African fish eagle is often called "the voice of Africa," and its Latin name, Haliaeetus vocifer, was most likely a result of its vocal presence. (Photo © Lynn M. Stone)

Above: Eagle image from a birchbark song scroll from the Algonquin people of the Canadian Great Lakes region.

SOARING BALD EAGLE
Proud symbol of the United States, the bald eagle has appeared on U.S. coins since 1776, when it first appeared on the Massachusetts copper. The first U.S. gold coins to carry the eagle's image were the "eagles," worth ten dollars, and "half-eagles," worth five dollars, minted in 1795. (Photo © Frank Oberle)

It is the eagle active, soaring in a wide, windy sky on a day of brilliant sunshine, that becomes transcendently the symbol of our freedom. Many years have passed since the day, but I remember vividly one such bird as it mounted above my canoe floating on a forest lake in the Adirondacks. With wings outspread, riding the updrafts in effortless ascent, white head and tail gleaming in the sun, it left the earth, the lake, the forest, the mountains behind. My paddle forgotten, I watched it recede into the shining sky of that August day. It shrank to sparrow size, this bird with a wingspan of nearly seven feet. As long as I could see it, it turned endlessly in spirals and graceful

curves, writing its poetry of motion on a blue page of the sky.

And from Frederick Kent Truslow comes "Eye to Eye with Eagles," published in *National Geographic* in 1961:

He is a bird of power, of self-reliance, and of majesty—a lover of freedom who effortlessly soars the air currents until he is but a speck in the sky. Master of the domain he surveys, he is not easily provoked. Cornered, he becomes a fury who will not willingly wear any man's shackles. What a tragedy if his kind should vanish from the earth!

AUDUBON IMAGE OF THE BALD EAGLE
Artist James Audubon, probably working from his observations on the Mississippi and Ohio Rivers, illustrated the bald eagle clutching a catfish in his The Birds of America.

Not everyone shares this view of the bald eagle as a noble lover of freedom. When the fledgling United States searched for a powerful national symbol, the Continental Congress chose the then-common and highly visible bald eagle, but there were dissenting opinions. John James Audubon, in *The Birds of America* (ca. 1840), quoted the views of one of the most respected men of that time:

"FOR MY PART," says [Benjamin Franklin], in one of his letters, "I wish the Bald Eagle had not been chosen as the representative of our country. He is a bird of bad moral character; he does not get his living honestly; you may have seen him perched on some dead tree, where, too lazy to fish for himself, he watches the labour of the Fishing-Hawk; and when that diligent bird has at length taken a fish, and is bearing it to his nest for the support of his mate and young ones, the Bald Eagle pursues him, and takes it from him. With all this injustice, he is never in good case, but, like those among men who live by sharing and robbing, he is generally poor, and often very lousy."

HUNTING STRATEGIES

*M*oralistic interpretations aside, Franklin was correct about the bald eagle's piratical habits. Many observers have watched a bald eagle swoop down upon a fish-laden osprey, deftly relieving the osprey of his load. One of the best descriptions of this feat, and of the bald eagle, comes from the writings of ornithologist Alexander Wilson (*American Ornithology*, 1808–1814):

FORMED BY NATURE for braving the severest cold; feeding equally on the produce of the sea and of the land; possessing powers of flight capable of outstripping even the tempests themselves; unawed by any thing but man; and, from the ethereal

FISHING BALD EAGLE *The bald eagle prefers fish, fresh or dead, and is skilled at snatching them from the water. Bald eagles have also been seen riding low in the water, "rowing" themselves toward shore with their wings, their talons securely hooked in a fish or waterfowl too big to carry off.*
(Photo © Tom & Pat Leeson)

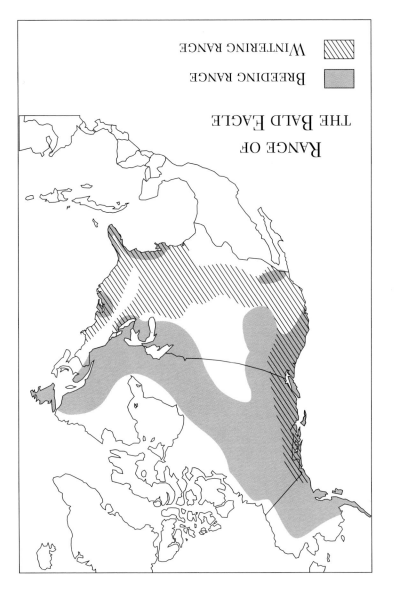

**RANGE OF
THE BALD EAGLE**

◻ **BREEDING RANGE**

▨ **WINTERING RANGE**

BALD EAGLE AND EAGLET

Eagles feed their young by ripping off morsels of meat and offering them to the eaglet, patiently trying again and again if refused. The gentleness of the great bird with its offspring has left many observers spellbound. (Photo © Tom & Pat Leeson)

heights to which he soars, looking abroad, at one glance, on an immeasurable expanse of forests, fields, lakes, and ocean, deep below him, he appears indifferent to localities and to change of seasons; as, in a few minutes, he can pass from summer to winter, from the lower to the higher regions of the atmosphere, the abode of eternal cold, and thence descend, at will, to the torrid, or the arctic regions of the earth. He is, therefore, found at all seasons in the countries he inhabits; but prefers such places as have been mentioned above, from the great partiality he has for fish.

In procuring these, he displays, in a very singular manner, the genius and energy of his character, which is fierce, contemplative, daring, and tyrannical—attributes not exerted but on particular occasions, but, when put forth, overpowering all opposition. Elevated on the high dead limb of some gigantic tree that commands a wide view of the neighboring shore and ocean, he seems calmly to contemplate the motions of the various feathered tribes that pursue their busy avocations below—the snow-white Gulls slowly winnowing the air; the busy *Tringæ*, coursing along the sands; trains of Ducks, streaming over the surface; silent and watchful Cranes, intent and wading; clamorous Crows; and all the winged multitudes that subsist by the bounty of this vast liquid magazine of nature. High over all these hovers one, whose action instantly arrests his whole attention. By his wide curvature of wing, and sudden suspension in air, he knows him to be the the Fish-Hawk settling over some devoted victim of the deep. His eye kindles at the sight, and balancing himself, with half-opened wings, on the branch, he watches the result. Down, rapid as an arrow from the heaven, descends the distant object of his attentions, the roar of its wings reaching the ear as it disappears in the deep, making the surges foam around. At this moment, the eager looks of the Eagle are all ardor; and leveling his neck for flight, he sees the Fish-Hawk once more emerge, struggling with his prey, and mounting in the air with screams of exultation. These are the signal for our hero, who, launching into the air, instantly gives chase, and soon gains on the Fish-Hawk; each exerts his utmost to mount above the other, displaying in these encounters the most elegant and sublime aerial evolutions. The unencumbered Eagle rapidly advances, and is just on the point of reaching his opponent, when, with a sudden scream, probably of despair and

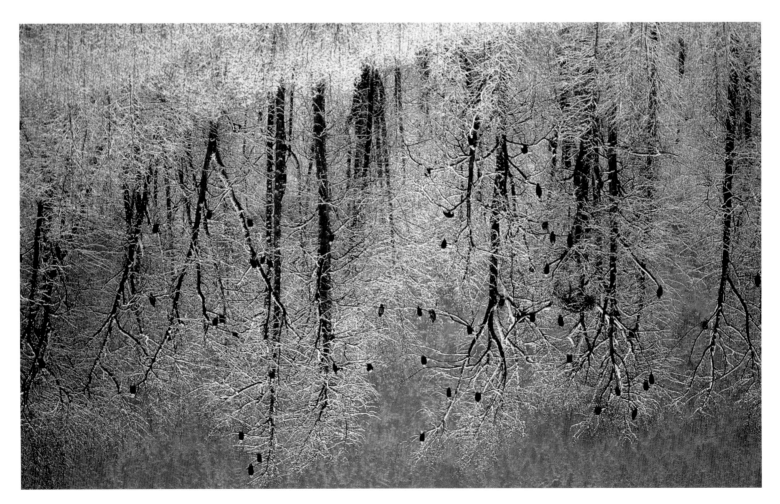

FLOCK OF BALD EAGLES
The Chilkat River in southeastern Alaska is an annual gathering ground for bald eagles, who come to feast on the last major run of spawning salmon. During October, November, and December, there may be 3,000 or more eagles feeding on dead and dying fish along several miles of river. Roosting in frost-covered trees along the river, the eagles form a spectacular tableau. (Photo © Jeff Foott)

honest execration, the latter drops his fish; the Eagle, poising himself for a moment, as if to take a more certain aim, descends like a whirlwind, snatches it in his grasp ere it reaches the water, and bears his ill-gotten booty silently away to the woods.

In *The Birds of America* (ca. 1830), Audubon, who on the subject of bald eagles falls more into Franklin's camp than Wilson's, described another method of hunting often used by bald eagles in pursuit of waterfowl:

AT TIMES, WHEN these Eagles, sailing in search of prey, discover a Goose, a Duck, or a Swan, that has alighted on the water, they accomplish its destruction in a manner that is worthy of your attention. The Eagles, well aware that water-fowl have it in their power to dive at their approach, and thereby elude their attempts upon them, ascend in the air in opposite directions over the lake or river, on which they have observed the object which they are desirous of possessing. Both eagles reach a certain height, immediately after which one of them glides with great swiftness towards the prey; the latter, mean-

BALD EAGLE MATES

When bald eagles come together, they use their voices to convey a variety of information. They may be warning an intruder from their territory or reassuring their mate as they come to the nest. In this case, the calling eagle seems to be stating its case for possession of its perch. (Photo © Henry H. Holdsworth)

time, aware of the Eagle's intention, dives the moment before he reaches the spot. The pursuer then rises in the air, and is met by its mate, which glides toward the water-bird, that has just emerged to breathe, and forces it to plunge again beneath the surface, to escape the talons of this second assailant. The first Eagle is now poising itself in the place where its mate formerly was, and rushes anew to force the quarry to make another plunge. By thus alternately gliding, in rapid and often repeated rushes, over the ill-fated bird, they soon fatigue it, when it stretches out its neck, swims deeply, and makes for the shore, in the hope of concealing itself among the rank weeds. But this is of no avail, for the Eagles follow it in all its motions, and the moment it approaches the margin, one of them darts upon it, and kills it in an instant, after which they divide the spoil.

A NEW GENERATION

Reaching maturity at four to five years of age, about the same time they acquire their full adult coloring, bald eagles select a mate and pair for several years, or even for life. Courtship flights much like those of the golden eagle help to cement the bond, and the pair begin to construct or refurbish a nest.

BALD EAGLES FIGHTING OVER PERCH
A choice perch can be the cause of many squabbles when many eagles are concentrated in an area. Such gatherings are usually the result of a local abundance of food, such as spawning salmon. (Photo © Henry H. Holdsworth)

Unlike most golden eagles, bald eagles prefer to nest in trees, often building immense structures over a period of several years. When trees or other suitable structures aren't available, such as on some Arctic islands, bald eagles will nest on the ground, although this obviously makes the nestlings more vulnerable to any ground-dwelling predators in the area.

Nesting and egg-laying times vary throughout the range of the bald eagle, occurring earlier and lasting longer in the south than in the north. Even so, a bald eagle pair arriving to set up housekeeping in Saskatchewan in April will usually sit out a few snowstorms hunkered down on the nest. Eventually, one to three eggs are laid, several days apart, and about thirty-five days later the incubating parent becomes aware of a change occurring beneath her.

The mother eagle may first be alerted by a soft peeping from within an egg. The chick inside will give this call throughout the struggle to escape from the egg, which can take twenty-four hours or more. Beginning by piercing the shell with its small, sharp, egg tooth, a bony projection on the upper part of its beak, the chick gradually enlarges the opening and finally emerges—wet, blind, and helpless. Its eyes will soon open and its pale beige-gray down will soon dry, but the eaglet will remain frail and dependent for some time.

Tended by solicitous parents who provide tasty morsels of fish, the eaglets have little to do but eat, sleep, and grow. Feathers gradually replace down until, when they are about eighty days old and about 98 percent of their adult size, the eaglets are ready to make their first flight. After that, it's not long until they join their parents, soaring over the land and water they have gazed upon from their nest.

ILL FORTUNES

When Europeans first came to the New World, bald eagles nested over a large part of North America—the southern limit of their range roughly marked by a line from Florida to Baja California, the northern by a line from Labrador to Alaska. Estimates of the total bald eagle population at that time range from 250,000 to 500,000, with about 25,000 to 50,000 living in the lower forty-eight states. Yet, as early as the late 1800s, observers were noting an absence of the birds in areas where they had once been common. By the early 1960s, fewer than 450 nesting pairs of bald eagles could be found in the lower forty-eight states.

What caused the terrible decline? The initial problem came from the fact that the quiet haunts of the eagle were invaded by first a trickle—then a flood—of "civilization," bringing humanity. By the early 1840s, Audubon (*The Birds of North America*) was already noticing a difference:

BEFORE STEAM NAVIGATION commenced on our western rivers, these Eagles were extremely abundant there, particularly in the lower parts of the Ohio, the Mississippi, and the adjoining streams. I have seen hundreds while going down from the mouth of the Ohio to New Orleans, when it was not at all difficult to shoot them. Now, however, their number is considerably diminished, the game on which they were in the habit of feeding, having been forced to seek refuge from the persecution of man farther in the wilderness.

Bald eagles are not tolerant of human presence near their nests and will abandon eggs and young if disturbed, so human encroachment was a serious problem. Call it "Strike One." And Audubon, seemingly unaware of the import of his words, also mentioned another human-caused problem for bald eagles—deliberate persecution. "Strike Two." The third strike came in the form of chemicals applied to the land in the post–World War II period. As organochlorides leached from the land accumulated to deadly levels in fish, bald eagles' main food source, the eagles laid eggs that broke or addled. Sometimes the toxins caused direct poisoning of the birds.

With three strikes against them, bald eagles were definitely on their way "out," and were officially declared endangered in 1967. The fact that they have recovered sufficiently to be reclassified as merely "threatened" in 1995 is also due to direct human intervention, this time in a positive way. By banning problem chemicals and reintroducing eagles into suitable areas, humans have worked hard to reverse some of the damage done.

So why is preserving these birds so important? Aside from any economic benefits derived from eco-tourism, or from the religious and monetary value placed on their feathers, bald eagles are of incalculable worth to humans simply for the joy of their beauty and the strength of their symbolism. Their "rusty hinge" voices are a clarion call to preserve North America's

A Tower of Bald Eagles

The Eagles are one of the oldest clans and strongest totems of the Haida people of the Queen Charlotte Islands, off the coast of British Columbia, Canada. This Haida story about bald eagles, recorded by ethnologist Marius Barbeau in *Haida Myths* (1953), tells of magic and of the ties of kinship:

One day long ago, as the chief's nephew was wading in the water at low tide, his feet unexpectedly were caught by . . . [a] monster Clam, who began to swallow him. An Eagle flew down to the young man, and grasping his shoulders, he tried to pull him out of the monster's clutch. But the rescuer too was dragged down. While the tide was swiftly rising, the Eagle kinsmen stood helpless and aggrieved on the shore. Another Eagle rushed to the assistance of the bird and the man, and was also pulled down into the sea. More Eagles from aloft scurried in vain to the rescue, holding each other up in a chain, until the old mother of all the Eagles used her magic powers and at last managed to save her brood and their human protégé.

Squadron of bald eagles
The Haida story of the Eagle People rescuing the son of a chief from a giant clam comes to life with this squadron of bald eagles. (Photo © Henry H. Holdsworth)

fast-vanishing wilderness. Unfortunately for bald eagles, and all raptors, peaceful existence is a tenuous pleasure, based on a commodity far less constant than the winds on which they ride—human values.

We would do well to remember what Alan Devoe wrote about the bald eagle in an article called "Down to Earth" (*American Mercury*, 1938). His words are as beautiful and as true today as they were then:

It is a superb and fascinating creature, this great-winged raptorian. . . . With wings outstretched it may cover a spread of more than seven feet, from the one tip to the other, and in flight it affords a spectacle of incomparable wild beauty. The man who has ever stood on the shore of a lonely lake, or in the twilit silence of a forest, and listened to the edged scream of an eagle whose haunt is there, will not quickly get the sound out of his ears.

Bald eagle perch
White head and tail gleaming in the sun like bright beacons, a bald eagle surveys its domain from a rocky perch. (Photo © David Welling)

Troubled Skies

Sometimes eagles' wings,
Unseen before by Gods or wondering men,
Darken'd the place.
—John Keats, "Hyperion: A Fragment"

BALD EAGLE AND FULL MOON
Facing page: *For thousands of years, eagles and humans have looked up at the same cold moon, our closest neighbor in the universe. We tend to forget that our planet is an isolated sanctuary, a safe haven shared with millions of other living creatures. If by our actions we harm or destroy this small island in space, neither eagles nor humans have anywhere else to go.* (Photo © Henry H. Holdsworth)

Above: *Eagle image from the art of Southwestern Native Americans.*

All eagles, along with other raptors, have suffered losses similar to those of the bald and golden eagles, carrying several species to the brink of extinction. How and why did this happen? The most basic answer points to two underlying causes: the human desire for simple solutions, and the homocentric nature of humans—we are much more concerned about the effect of our actions on human interests than about their effect on other living creatures. In 1962, Rachel Carson, in a book called *Silent Spring*, alerted the world to the terrible chemical havoc that we were unintentionally wreaking on our world. From that book comes this still-true passage, describing the human tendency to oversimplify nature:

IN SOME QUARTERS nowadays it is fashionable to dismiss the balance of nature as a state of affairs that prevailed in an earlier, simpler world—a state that has now been so thoroughly upset that we might as well forget it. Some find this a convenient assumption, but as a chart for a course of action it is highly dangerous. The balance of nature is not the same today as in Pleistocene times, but it is still there: a complex, precise, and highly integrated system of relationships between living things which cannot safely be ignored any more than the law of gravity can be defied with impunity by a man perched on the edge of a cliff. The balance of nature is not a status quo; it is a fluid, ever shifting, in a constant state of adjustment. Man, too, is a part of this balance. Sometimes the balance is in his favor; sometimes—and all too often through his own activities—it is shifted to his disadvantage.

Humans are unique. No other species has the power to so dramatically change the planet we inhabit. No other species is guided in its actions, as humans often are, by a combination of popular opinion, greed, and lack of knowledge. These singular traits have proven unfortunate for a good portion of the earth's ecology and particularly deadly for eagles.

The Handbook of the Birds of the World (1994) remarked on the fatal effects of changing attitudes:

THE UNPRECEDENTED REVERENCE offered to raptors through falconry in Europe's Middle Ages was suddenly and dramatically replaced towards the end of the eighteenth century by an obsession, at least as strong, to destroy these same birds which were soon to be labelled "vermin"! This change in human attitudes towards raptors occurred as early as the sixteenth century in parts of England, and overseas emigrants carried with them this new and hostile approach to predators. Prior to this, they had mostly been regarded with indifference, and had been eliminated only locally, when they did persistent damage to free-range poultry, which is still the way they are treated today in many Third World countries. But now they were regarded as enemies, because of their supposed competition with human interests. With the changes in people's ways of thinking, they were also increasingly considered as rapacious and cruel beings: few people knew them enough to admire their beauty or admire their usefullness. . . . The potential benefits brought about by the predatory activities of raptors, such as their controlling of agricultural pests, checking the spread of diseases, and maintaining the balance in nature, were ignored or thought greatly to underweigh their grossly exaggerated or misinterpreted depredations.

The wars of destruction raged at their fiercest between 1860 and 1960. Most developed countries finally began enacting protective legislation between 1960 and 1980. Laws fail to de-

ter some of the most determined killers, however, who continue to take their toll each year with gun, trap, and poison.

CAMPAIGNS OF DESTRUCTION

The killing of eagles as vermin was led by European game keepers and sheep farmers. When guns alone proved unsatisfactory, gamekeepers used poisoned carcasses and traps to kill every eagle they could find. Right alongside marched the sheep farmer. Together these two groups robbed or destroyed nests and their occupants.

Modern studies show that eagle predation is a negligible factor in sheep mortality, as eagles usually take only the dead or the nearly departed. Some farmers realized this and also knew that eagles consumed rabbits and ground squirrels that competed with their livestock for forage. These farmers allowed the eagles to live at peace on their land. However, to most farmers with sheep, the only good eagle was a dead eagle. One would like to think that this was all history, turn-of-the-century folly that could be blamed on simple lack of knowledge. But as George Laycock learned, when writing *Autumn of the Eagle* (1973), even that minimal comfort is denied us:

IN THE AUTUMN of 1970 [James O.] Vogan [of the Buffalo Flying Service in Buffalo, Wyoming] was dispatched, with a helicopter to the ranch of Herman Werner, near Casper, Wyoming. Vogan testified [in later federal hearings] that his assignment was to fly the rangeland and kill predators, for which Buffalo Flying Service was to be paid a flat fee, with each dead eagle worth $25.

Vogan, as pilot, did not customarily perform the actual executions. His hands were full maneuvering the helicopter to keep his gunner in range of the birds as the eagles attempted to escape. . . . On some occasions the gunner would be an employee of the Buffalo Flying Service. But ordinarily Vogan could obtain free help by finding gunners around town or on the ranches, where there always seemed to be someone eager to go along and do the shooting.

"Did he pay the gunners?" Senator McGee asked. "Why would the others go out and freeze their fingers and feet?"

"For the enjoyment of it," Vogan replied. He also testified that invariably the gunners were told that the operation was

74

CROWDS AT THE FEAST

Bald eagles gather to feast on dead or dying spawned-out salmon. Active fish, working their way upstream to spawn, are still quite strong, and the eagles prefer to do the minimum amount of work necessary to eat. Although eagles and seals had been feeding on salmon for hundreds of years before humans came, they were blamed for the severe drop in fish stocks that occurred after several years of commercial fishing. The Alaskan bald eagle bounty was a direct result of this scapegoating and encouraged the killing of more than 100,000 bald eagles. (Photo © Henry H. Holdsworth)

covered by permits making it legal for them to kill eagles. . . .

Vogan reports that the bald eagle . . . proved far more difficult to shoot down. "The Golden Eagle, I would say, is not really a hard bird to zero in on and get your gunner in position to shoot, but a Bald Eagle, if you shoot a Bald Eagle down, I can guarantee you, you earn your money." Vogan testified that he had, "seen as high as a box of shells shot up on one eagle." He found the eagle to be a "tough bird," and added that, "even if they look dead, you had better get out and kick them and make sure, and you better have a gun or something to protect yourself." . . .

The best days for the gunners, according to Vogan, were windy days, when eagles would leave their perches and soar effortlessly on the updrafts. By the time one bird was shot from the sky the next victim was often already in view. One day Vogan and his gunner killed 29 eagles, another day 31, and on one especially rewarding day, 36 of the giant birds. As he flew, Vogan tried to remember his score until he landed and could make a hurried entry in his notebook: "We were shooting so many down it would be almost impossible to keep track of them from memory."

There was good reason for writing down the kill. This was the tally sheet by which his employer collected his executioner's fees: $50 per coyote and $25 per eagle. . . . For its predator killing services, Werner is believed to have paid Buffalo Flying Service at least $15,000.

Jon Gerrard and Gary Bortolotti (*The Bald Eagle*, 1988) commented on the same campaign of destruction:

IT IS ESTIMATED that 20,000 eagles, mostly Goldens but some Balds, were killed to save lambs between 1950 and 1970. Most were shot by hired guns who went up in airplanes. One wonders how high the price of lamb could be to justify such an expense. Or did it become more the love of a blood sport that drove people to such acts?

The deliberate and unnecessary slaughter of golden and bald eagles in the American West is one of the blackest marks on the conservation record. Much of this activity was paid for by sheep ranchers, who also added to the toll through the use of poison baits, mainly intended for coyotes, but killing incidental "bonus" eagles as well. The ranchers had some powerful help. In 1970, the Division of Wildlife Services put out their own Borgia banquet: 10,800 baits laced with deadly, nonspecific 1080 (sodium monofluoracetate) poison; 805,000 strychnine baits; 32,933 cyanide "coyote getters." The destruction of nontarget wildlife, such as eagles, was known to be a problem, and George Laycock, in *Autumn of the Eagle* (1973), described how one regional supervisor cautioned his field men to take care placing baits, because dead eagles were an "embarrassment to the Bureau." His suggestion was to wait to place baits until casual foot traffic through the area had diminished, lessening the possibility of a hiker coming across an eagle carcass. Just as an aside, all this was happening even though bald and golden eagles had been protected in the United States since 1962.

Earlier in the century, a place often thought of as a haven for wildlife, Alaska, relentlessly slaughtered the bald eagle— for dubious reasons. In a 1928 article for the *North American Review* entitled "Blood Money for Eagles," Arthur Newton Pack wrote:

TO THE SERIOUS student of wild life no phase of human activity is more patent than man's tendency to blame some other creatures for depleted conditions that he has brought about by his own destructive methods. There is a regrettable fashion of jumping to conclusions, and urging the wholesale destruction of supposedly injurious creatures without any adequate preliminary study of the factors in the case. This tendency is unfortunately all too prevalent in our treatment of many of our most beautiful and useful species, and leads to many notable abuses. Much of this is due to a reluctance to interfere with established methods of business that came into being a generation or more ago, when the impending decline of many of our most valuable species, valuable from both commercial and aesthetic considerations, was unsuspected. . . . Eagles are notoriously heavy eaters of fish, but we believe that it has nowhere been denied that the bulk of those eaten in Alaska are dead or dying fish that have worn themselves out in the struggle to fight their way to the spawning grounds. It is a well-known fact that the salmon fisheries have been over-exploited for many

TAWNY EAGLE ON POWER POLE
As this tawny eagle in India shows, eagles like to use power poles as vantage points. Electrocution is a major cause of death for eagles because their broad wings can make a fatal connection between two wires. Solutions to the problem include burying power lines and placing either safe perching platforms or devices that deter perching on top of the poles. (Photo © Göran Ekström/Windrush Photos)

years, and that the blame for the continued scarcity has been laid to the depredations of various creatures, bulls, tern, sea-lions, and now—the eagle.

In 1965 her book, *Raccoons and Eagles*, Polly Redford gave her views on the situation in Alaska:

AFTER FIFTY YEARS of the white man's fishing methods there were fewer salmon in the rivers than before, so the white men naturally blamed the eagles.

Bald eagles were also hated by fur farmers who had stocked small islands with commercially valuable blue foxes which they fed and allowed to run free for two or three years before trapping and selling them on the market. The foxes throve on these islands and soon overran them completely, killing off large numbers of seabirds that lied along the shores. No longer able to prey upon these birds, some of the resident bald eagles turned to blue fox cubs instead.

And so a bounty on bald eagles was passed by the territorial legislature in 1917, based on a firm conviction that it would help local business.

Between 1917 and 1953, more than 100,000 bald eagles were killed and turned in for the Alaskan bounty. What was this great reward? In 1917, a pair of eagle claws fetched fifty cents. By 1953, they were worth two dollars. The price we, and future generations, have really paid may never be known.

As Herbert Ravenal Sass was well aware (*On the Wings of a Bird*, 1929), there are even less savory reasons for killing eagles than simple monetary gain:

WHEN WE SEE the . . . eagle in life, standing aloof and watchful on some lofty vantage point or sailing on wide motionless pinions through the air, too often the gun leaps to the shoulder, and the great bird comes whirling down, a blood-spattered mass of carrion.

Why? The answer is simple.

The eagle is a big bird, a very big bird, and we shoot all very big birds that come our way. Moreover, he is, in most parts of the country, something of a rarity, and it is considered quite a feat to kill and bring home so huge and strange a creature. Everybody is interested and scores of people crowd around the carcass and marvel at the vast spread of wing and the long, sharp claws. We are pointed out as the mighty Nimrod who did the deed. We puff out our chest; and great is our pride when we read a story in the paper next day that Mr. So-and-So, one of the most enthusiastic of local sportsmen, killed an eagle measuring seven feet from tip to tip, and how the great bird, the first one seen in that region in years, created a sensation when its body was exhibited at Jones and Brown's store.

DEAD BALD EAGLE
This bald eagle may have died from any number of causes, most of them traceable back to human activities. Chemical residues in the food chain, deliberate shooting or poisoning, oil spills, habitat destruction that ruins both hunting and nesting grounds—human interaction with eagles and their world is often detrimental to the eagles. (Photo © Jeff Foott)

In *Raccoons and Eagles* (1965), Polly Redford agreed: "Hawks and eagles make exciting targets for weekend Daniel Boone's trying out their mail-order shotguns, the kind of hunters whose constitutional right to bear arms is exercised on road signs and stray cats."

THE COLLECTORS

It is difficult to look back on people in the past without judging their actions by our current moral standards. For example, the hobby of collecting bird's eggs (oology) and bird skins was quite respectable at the turn of the century. Unfortunately, it was the feverish acquisitiveness of these collectors that provided the final coup de grace for the white-tailed sea eagles in Great Britain. Already pushed to their limits by gamekeepers and sheep farmers, the eagles couldn't withstand the sustained attack on their population. The oologists knew that white-tailed sea eagles at that time still commonly bred in Iceland, Greenland, and Scandinavia, and they thought that these birds would come to replenish their stocks. What they didn't know was that eagles have strong bonds to the place where they hatch and fledge—the far-off eagles did not come to Great Britain.

In the United States, for many years, it was considered a great thing to have a stuffed eagle to display in your store, school, lodge, or meeting hall—even as eagles became scarce in the wild. In *The Bald Eagle* (1988), Jon Gerrard and Gary Bortolotti quote a 1919 poem by Henry W. Shoemaker that makes the irony clear:

Suspended by a dirty string
In a dingy down-town store
With wings wide-spread
A stuffed Bald Eagle hangs
And as the summer breezes blow
Filth-laden through a small window
The regal bird, which once did soar
Above the clouds, above the storm
Swings gently round and round.

Today, another kind of collector helps to fuel a brisk black market in eagle body parts and feathers. Buyers of Indian ceremonial objects want authenticity and, while some makers of these articles are responsibly using substitutes, such as dyed turkey feathers, others are using eagle parts obtained illegally. Each year poachers take their toll on legally protected birds. This is not a new craze. Such is the popularity of eagles that, in the early 1960s before eagles were protected, Boy Scouts were making neckerchief slides from eagle talons and headdresses from eagle feathers—until the Audubon Society explained to them what using these materials meant for the eagles.

The collecting spirit is also taking its toll elsewhere. In parts of Latin America, a pet or stuffed raptor, particularly an eagle, is still considered a status symbol. In southeast and eastern Asia, it's the same story—with the additional desire to use the birds as delicacies or medicine. Rarity, of course, merely adds to the price. The human urge to collect is a strong one that must be tempered with common sense. Countless eggs, lying in glass cases with neat labels, are nothing but sad promises, unfulfilled. The dusty corpses of wild animals, killed because of their beauty, tell us little of their living grace and power. We can only hope that, over time, education will stop this kind of senseless slaughter. Tragically, many of the endangered eagles have already given us just about all the time they have left.

Indirect and Unintentional

Direct persecution isn't the only way in which humans have had a negative impact on eagles. Destruction of habitat threatens eagles and many other species on this small planet. Protecting eagles serves very little purpose unless we also preserve a place for them to live in peace.

Growing human populations continuously encroach on undeveloped areas, replacing wetlands and forests with subdivisions and strip malls, turning quiet shorelines into bustling marinas. Farmers working to squeeze every last cent from their land remove bush and fill sloughs. Outdoor enthusiasts shatter the stillness of lakes with powerboats and jet skis. Logging activities disturb nesting birds and sometimes destroy nest trees. Curious people, ignorant of the consequences of their actions, repeatedly disturb eagles on the nest.

Our insatiable need for electricity causes eagles to die by the hundreds annually from electrocution, their broad wings making a fatal bridge between powerlines. Electrocution is the cause of death for 15 percent of young Bonelli's eagles in France each year. Eagles are also killed by flying into the blades of wind turbines, a "green" energy source. These deaths are caused unintentionally, but they are no less real.

Perhaps the most tragic and far-reaching of human legacies is the contamination of our air, land, and water with the residues of our love affair with technology. Like a child with a new chemistry set, we were so enthralled with the success of that great all-purpose insecticide, DDT, that we sprayed with gleeful abandon. We tried it on everything we could think of and saw dramatic results. It appeared to be efficient and cost-effective. In reality, the cost was more than anyone could have imagined. *The Handbook of the Birds of the World* (1994) gives this description of the situation:

IN THE 1950's, the rapidly increasing use of DDT and other persistent organochlorines to control agricultural pests and mosquitoes, or in seed dressings, resulted in the extensive poisoning of insectivorous and granivorous birds, and consequently of their predators. Raptor breeding success was severely affected. Besides cases of acute poisoning and direct mortality, pesticide contamination and the magnification of residues up the food chain, resulted in the accumulation of sub-lethal levels of chemicals, and in the breeding failure of raptors through eggshell thinning, egg breakage and embryo deaths. This led, in turn, to widespread and serious population declines.

Widely used and often applied aerially in great swaths, these chemicals washed down into streams, rivers, lakes, and estuaries and found their way into the aquatic food chain. Concentrated in tissues of fish, the toxic residues made their way to the aerie. Here, they could cause the death of the young or parent bird directly, or cause them to become too weak to stave off other attacks on their systems. Even more insidiously, these chemicals caused nest failure by acting on the hormonal system of the female eagle, so she laid eggs with shells too fragile to survive brooding. Raptor populations crashed. Everywhere, bird-watchers and bird banders sounded the alarm. In the late 1950s and early 1960s, as the enormity of what was happening became clear, environmentally aware people pushed to get DDT banned. In 1962, a book called *Silent Spring* gave us a new hero, Rachel Carson, and the call to ban DDT gained strength. Not until 1972 did the United States ban DDT and, although some countries followed suit, DDT is still used in some parts of the world. Since the 1960s, new chemical hazards have been recognized: PCBs, DDE, heptachlor epoxide, and dieldrin — all of which have been found in eagle eggshells from the Great Lakes region. The global threat posed by PCB and DDT residues may be the most worrying, but other poisons, such as mercury, continue to add to the death toll.

Another chemical hazard for eagles, and other animals, is lead poisoning caused by ingesting shot. When an eagle eats a hunter-crippled duck, it gets not only a meal, but also an unwelcome dose of lead from the pellets lodged in the duck's flesh. If it eats enough of these ducks, the eagle will die. In some areas, lead poisoning from shot is considered a significant cause of eagle mortality. Because of this, and because of the deaths of other birds, such as swans, who inadvertently scoop up fallen shot when feeding on bottom vegetation, the United States banned the use of lead shot for waterfowl hunting in 1991. Canada dragged its feet on the issue, but in 1995, finally announced a ban that applied to national wildlife areas in 1996 and became nationwide in 1997.

THE FUTURE?

Reintroduction programs have helped to bring raptors, including the peregrine falcon and the bald eagle, back to areas from which they had disappeared, but the witches' brew of residues still in the system continues to be a problem. George Laycock (*Autumn of the Eagle*, 1973) clearly described the plight of today's eagles:

AS THE TOTAL numbers decline, the death of an individual eagle assumes an increasing seriousness in relation to the remaining population. Today's eagles survive in a chamber of horrors. The hunting parent lifts a sick fish from the water and with it carries along to the nest a new portion of chemical insecticides. And fish may be attached to a tangle of tough monofilament fishing line, in which the young become entangled and die. Another eagle, a young inexperienced bird, meanwhile falls victim to an automobile. Others drop before thoughtless gunners, are caught in traps, or are methodically executed by sheepmen using poisons, shotguns, traps, and airplanes.

More insidious than these recognizable hazards are the invisible pressures exerted on the remaining eagles: stresses from crowding, noise, and environmental pollution, some of them only speculative, inconclusive, and not measurable. There are other factors that can only be revealed by sophisticated chemical analysis of the tissues, among them DDT, DDE, PCBs, and heavy metals. Whether one such agent alone brings death to the individual eagle or they combine in some unfathomed mixture scarcely matters. Total pressures upon the eagles are overwhelming.

There are flickers of light in all this darkness. We have been acting to set aside land for eagles and the other species that share their world. We are working to save those eagles that have been pushed to the edge of extinction — captive breeding programs, brood manipulation of Cain and Abel species, and, in extreme cases, armed guards at nests are fighting to keep us from losing birds like the Philippine Eagle forever. Some countries and companies are spending extra money to bury power-lines or to build safe nesting platforms on transmission towers. Increasing pressure to clean up our water and air is forcing needed changes. We have made progress. We must make more.

BALD EAGLES ON DEAD TREE
Sharing a convenient perch, a group of bald eagles appear to form a living totem pole. Strong symbols in many cultures, eagles should be treasured by all people and given space to live. (Photo © Tom & Pat Leeson)

BANDING EAGLES

One of the ways to help eagles is to learn more about them, and one way to do this is to band young eagles in the nest. Information obtained while at the nest—about diet items, parasites, nest success—can be invaluable. And when bands are later recovered from dead birds, information about travel patterns and lifespan is gained

A retired Canadian banker turned bald eagle bander in Florida, Charles Broley, was one of the first to raise the alarm over the effects of DDT. Having begun banding in 1939, Broley became aware in 1947 that nest success was low compared with other years. By 1952, things were so bad that, where he had banded 150 eaglets in 105 nests in 1939, Broley could find only 15 eaglets in 11 nests. He strongly suspected a link to heavy pesticide use, and his observations alerted others, starting the flood of protest that eventually caused DDT to be banned.

Each time a band is recovered, a bander has mixed feelings. On the one hand, there is the new information gained, and on the other, there is the knowledge that there is one less eagle flying. Of course, not everyone sees it that way. Montana journalist Gary Turbak ("America's Other Eagle," *National Wildlife*, 1989) described a conversation that took place several years ago between biologist Bart O'Gara and some Texas ranchers. "O'Gara lamented that most eagle legbands are never returned. The bands, he explained, could add to understanding of eagle migrations and predatory habits. A rancher later sauntered up to O'Gara and asked if he wanted some bands from golden eagles. "I got a 2-quart jar full of em at home," drawled the rancher."

Even with this kind of discouragement, banders persist, risking life and limb on unsound branches and wobbly ladders, dangling from ropes, suffering the pain of the occasional talon puncture or the greater pain of finding not healthy eaglets but broken or addled eggs. Not only do eagles get banded, but the people on whose land they nest become aware that they have something precious to be guarded and respected. Landowners uncertain about the operation may be invited to come see "their" eagles banded and learn by observing the banders that, although a very brief visit at this particular time by responsible, authorized people will not harm the eagles, the nest should be left strictly alone at other times. Afterwards, during conversations over coffee at the kitchen table, new knowledge about eagles may be gained by both groups.

A DAY IN THE LIFE OF AN EAGLE BANDER

What happens when bander meets eagle? This story of David Miller's, adapted from his banding diary, gives you a taste of what's involved in getting those precious bands in place.

THE FIRST BALD Eagle nest on the shore of Montreal Lake is mine. The mother lifts off the nest as we beach the boat and circles at a respectful distance. I am spurred and belted, and the climb up the old poplar is pretty straightforward for forty feet until I reach the crotch which supports the enormous nest. This massive structure must be five feet across and six feet deep and it takes fifteen minutes of sweat and struggle and false starts before I find a way to get up and over the edge while keeping at least one safety rope strung around something solid.

My solution is to get a leg up around a branch on the outside of the nest, and swing myself around and up onto the nest itself, ending up seated, facing outwards with the branch held—firmly—between my legs. I've had no thought for the birds during this process, as the climbing takes all my concentration, but I look around now and discover that (a) the two young eagles perching on the other side of the nest are tall enough to look me in the eye and (b) I'm sitting on a dead fish. Bird banding is a thrill.

I grab for the nearest eaglet, which spreads its wings to a breathtaking span of over six feet, and rewards my audacity with a vigorous buffeting about the face. I manage to rescue my glasses before they spin off into the void, and we both retire to our respective corners. On my next attempt, the eaglet neatly rips off my wristwatch. On the third try, I get hold of a leg and press the bird gently

BANDING EAGLES
The numbered metal band David Miller is placing on this golden eagle chick's leg will remain with it for life. When the eagle eventually dies, information about the eagle's age and range can be gained if the band is recovered. (Photo © Glen & Rebecca Grambo)

down onto the nest, folding its wings, and holding it so that it can hurt neither me nor itself while I secure the riveted band. Now for eaglet number two.

It's an even match: the eaglet lunges for me as I lunge for it and we both grab each other. As I catch the eaglet by both legs, the eaglet sinks all eight talons into my thigh.

"Nice Eagle," I lie reassuringly through my clenched teeth. I switch to the truth: "The quicker we're done, the happier we'll both be." The bird responds by smacking me in the face with an enormous wing. After a brief struggle, the band is on and I manage to pry open those great feet without injuring the eagle or adding to my own wounds.

As I sit drenched in sweat, I look across at my adversaries with their wings outstretched and threatening. "You guys are wonderful," I tell them with all sincerity. "Have a good life!" I hope these bands aren't recovered for a long, long time.

In Memoriam—A Partial Roll Call of the Victims

A single Scottish estate at Glengarry (1837–1840): 98 peregrines, 78 merlins, 462 kestrels, 285 buzzards, 3 honey buzzards, 15 golden eagles, 27 white-tailed eagles, 18 ospreys, 63 goshawks, 275 kites, and 68 harriers

Norway (1846–1900): 223,487 raptors, including 61,157 golden and white-tailed eagles up to 1869; 27,319 eagles from 1870–99

Iceland (1880–1921): poison baits put out for other species reduced the number of white-tailed eagles from 150 pairs to 7, without noticeable impact on the "target" species

Netherlands (1852–1857): 219 eagles (39,233 raptors)

Norway (1900–1966): approximately 500,000 raptors

Alaska (1917–1952): 128,273 bald eagles

Western Australia (1928–1968): 147,237 wedge-tailed eagles

Denmark (1942–1967): approximately 300,000 raptors

France (1950–1970): 100,000–300,000 raptors annually

Germany, Nordrhein-Westfalen districts (1951–1968): 210,520 raptors

New York State (1980): the male of the state's last natural, wild-breeding pair of bald eagles was shot

South Dakota (1981–1983): 200–300 bald eagles killed near one wildlife refuge, most caught in baited traps or shot on their night roosts

John Casparis, Alpine, Texas: "champion" eagle-killer; reported slaughtering up to 25 golden eagles in one day, over 1,000 eagles in one year, and a total of 12,000 golden and bald eagles over a twenty-year period

Fishing eagle

As this eagle plucks a fish from the water and carries it back to the aerie, does it bring death as well? Residues from pesticides like the infamous DDT accumulate in the tissues of fish, reducing or eliminating the ability of birds that feed on them to reproduce, or even killing the birds directly by poisoning them. (Photo © Frank Oberle)

The Essence of Eagles

When thou seest an Eagle, thou seest a portion of Genius; lift up thy head!
—William Blake, "The Marriage of Heaven and Hell"

In our attempts to impose order on the cosmos, what role do we assign to eagles? Our attitudes toward these remarkable birds have changed drastically through the centuries. In the beginning, eagles were associated with the gods, the sun, and the journey of souls. No other birds, with the possible exception of the great condors, have been universally given such exalted status and treated with such reverence. Eagles could fly to the sun, visit the kingdoms far above us, transport the spirits of departed warriors to their place in the heavens. Who could fail to recognize their power?

BIRDS OF THE GODS

Soaring flight made eagles a natural addition to the list of inhabitants of the upper kingdoms. The Germanic peoples named the eagle Odin's bird. An eagle was the right-hand bird of the Greek god Zeus, acting as messenger and even as procurer when Zeus desired the presence of young Ganymede. Zeus himself often took the shape of an eagle when seeking human females for companionship. Romans contin-

SILHOUETTE OF AN
AFRICAN FISH EAGLE
Facing page: Eagles have been linked with the sun since humans first watched their soaring flight. Silhouetted by fiery light, this African fish eagle embodies the solar eagle. (Photo © Stan Osolinski/The Green Agency)

Above: Eagle image from the Tlingit people of Alaska.

ued the symbolism, associating eagles with Jove, their version of Zeus. They believed that a general fortunate enough to see an eagle before a battle would be victorious.

The giant, eaglelike Roc, sometimes known as the Ruc or Rukh, appears in Persian legends and various folktales from the East. Interestingly enough, in Deuteronomy, chapter 32, the God of Israel is compared to an eagle and repeatedly called the "Rock." Etymologist Harold Bagley felt this could be explained by the gradual change from the eagle-headed Assyrian god, Nisroch, to the "One Light, the Great Fire," *oniseroch*, transferring some of the "eagleness" of the old god to the new one.

EAGLES AND THE SUN

*T*he strong link between eagles and the sun can be traced through many cultures. The Aztecs told how during the creation of the present world, the eagle and the jaguar fought over who would have the honor of becoming the sun. The eagle settled the matter by flinging himself into a fire and, thus, becoming the sun. The jaguar, following close behind, settled for becoming the moon, with the spots on his coat showing that he had been only partially burned. In light of this tale, it's easy to see why the Aztec eagle and jaguar warrior societies were considered the most elite of the military orders. The Aztecs also tied the eagle to the sun in another way, comparing the daily journey of the all-important sun to an eagle's flight: rising on the warming air of morning and swooping down out of sight at night in pursuit of prey.

The eagle plays a crucial role in the sun dance of the Plains peoples of North America, and symbolizes the sun in the rites of some of the Southwestern tribes. The Iroquois tell of Keneu, the golden eagle, and of Oshadagea, the giant eagle with a lake of dew on his back who lives in the western sky. This Iroquois poem, quoted in *The Return of the Sea Eagle* by John A. Love (1983) appears to tell of Keneu:

> *I hear the eagle bird*
> *With his great feathers spread,*
> *Pulling the blanket back from the east,*
> *How swiftly he flies,*
> *Bearing the sun to the morning.*

On the other side of the Atlantic arose a belief about the eagle and the sun that persisted for many centuries. The eagle was thought to be the only animal capable of looking directly into the sun. Aristotle and Pliny wrote of this and added that the eagle tested its young by facing them to the sun, rejecting any that looked away. The writers of early bestiaries, such as the twelfth-century *Book of Beasts*, added to the eagle's mystery by giving it the power of eternal youth:

WHEN THE EAGLE grows old and his wings become heavy and his eyes become darkened with a mist, then he goes in search of a fountain, and, over against it, he flies up to the height of heaven, even into the circle of the sun, and there he singes his wings and at the same time evaporates the fog of his eyes in a ray of the sun. Then at length taking a header down into the fountain, he dips himself three times in it, and instantly he is renewed with a great vigour of plumage and splendour of vision.

—Stephen Friar, *A Dictionary of Heraldry*, quoting the translation of T. H. White

Christians adopted this symbolism, comparing the eagle looking into the sun to Christ looking at His Father, and the renewal of the eagle's youth through its plunge into the fountain to the renewal of the soul through baptism. Even today, an eagle may be spied on the baptismal fonts in some older churches.

EAGLES AND DEATH

*W*hen the Roman emperor Augustus died in A.D. 14, his body, with appropriately imposing decorations and accompaniments, was carried to the Campus Martius. There a towering pyramidal funeral pyre had been built, and the emperor was placed upon it. As the torch was applied to the base of the pyre, men in the surrounding crowd cast their adornments into the flames. The flames crept upward and an eagle was released from the summit of the burning mound, symbolizing the ascent of Augustus's soul to the gods.

Others also associated eagles with death and the journey of souls. Welsh legend told of how the souls of brave warriors flew to heaven in the form of eagles. In ancient Sumer, the

BALD EAGLE GATHERING
Perhaps inspired by a sight such as this, many northern people have stories about villages of eagle people who can transform themselves into humans by removing their feather cloaks. (Photo © Frank Oberle)

MARTIAL EAGLE

The striking martial eagle (Polemaetus bellicosus) *is the largest African eagle, with females weighing around 13 pounds (5.9 kg). Its favorite foods include guineafowl and monitor lizards.* (Photo © Gerry Ellis/Ellis Nature Photography)

eagle brought new souls (children) to this world and carried departed souls to the underworld. In Syria, the eagle carried souls to its master, the sun. The Hopi in the southwestern United States believed that the dead rose to become clouds drifting in an eagle-ruled sky. In some cases, those who died could be reborn not just as clouds but as eaglets. The Hopi kept captive golden eagles, believing them to be messengers that could take their prayers to the spirits.

Eagles played the role of soul-bearers for many ancient cultures. Others associated them with death, too, but in different ways. The Aztecs identified the eagle with the sun and with one of the main ways of nourishing the sun—human sacrifice. The hearts of sacrificial victims were often placed in a stone vessel called the *cuauhxicalli*, which means "eagle gourd vessel." In central Mexico, eagle down became a common symbol of sacrifice.

The Zulus and other peoples of South Africa link the bateleur with battles and the ensuing carnage. One of their names for the bateleur translates as "eater of the warriors," which could be more factual than symbolic—one of the bateleur's main food sources is carrion. Other eagles share the same eating habits and reputation. A twelfth-century writer, Giraldus

Cambrensis, described an eagle sitting on Mount Snowdon, Wales, as a prophetess of war who fed on the dead and had "almost perforated the stone by cleaning and sharpening her bill."

A DYNAMIC RELATIONSHIP

*A*ncient peoples saw the relationship between humans and eagles as a dynamic one. In many stories, eagles interact directly with people, often testing them in some way and giving gifts if the tests are passed. Danish polar explorer Knud Rasmussen, in one of the stories from his 1932 book, *The Eagle's Gift*, relates a tale told by Alaskan Eskimo Sagluag about a particularly precious gift given in "a time when men knew no joy. Their whole life was work, food, digestion, and sleep. One day went by like another. They toiled, they slept, they awoke again to toil. Monotony rusted their minds."

A COUPLE LIVING in these days had three young sons, all showing promise of being excellent hunters and of providing for the couple when they became old. Tragedy struck when the eldest and then the middle son failed to come home from hunting. The family grieved but the youngest son, Ermine, soon began hunting too. One day, he saw a huge young eagle that flew down and landed nearby. The eagle pulled off its hood and turned into a young man.

The eagle told Ermine that unless Ermine promised to hold a festival of song when he got home, the eagle would kill him as he had Ermine's two brothers. Ermine agreed to hold the festival but told the eagle that he didn't know what a festival of song was. The eagle replied, "If you follow me, my mother will teach you what you don't understand. Your two brothers scorned the gifts of song and merrymaking; they would not learn, so I killed them."

Given this encouragement, Ermine agreed to follow and off they went. High into the mountains climbed Ermine and the eagle-man. As they approached the mountain top, a strange throbbing noise filled Ermine's ears and he asked the eagle what it was. "It is the beating of my mother's heart."

The eagle's mother, old and weak, waited inside. During the following days, under her instruction, Ermine and the eagle built a large feast hall, learned to sing songs, and beat upon a drum in rhythm with the music. Finally she showed them how to dance. At last the eagle returned Ermine to his people. Ermine set about fulfilling his promise to the mother eagle.

The people built a feast hall like the eagles' and stored up the meat of caribou and sea creatures in preparation for the celebration. Ermine and the others sang songs made up of their best and oldest memories set to music. They were accompanied on drums and tambourines made of wood and caribou hides. The joyous music and rhythm of the drumbeats moved the people to dance.

Many northern cultures have similar stories of how eagles gave the gift of music and dance to humans, sometimes describing the drumbeats as an imitation of the Eagle Mother's heart. Often the tale ends with the Eagle Mother becoming young again, her vigor renewed by the joy of the dance.

In all of their dealings with eagles, the ancient peoples maintained a respectful mien, acknowledging the connections between humans and the natural world, as well as the eagle's supernatural power. As people established permanent settlements and began to raise livestock, however, their attitude toward eagles changed. The powerful birds were now seen as threats to often precarious livelihoods, and the stories about them grew darker.

The Baila people of southcentral Africa have a story that reflects the increasingly uneasy relationship between humans and eagles. This version is based on one that appears in *African Folktales and Sculptures* (1952):

A WOMAN WHO worked in the fields often took her child with her and let it sleep in the shade while she hoed the crops. One day, the mother heard her child's fretful crying suddenly cease and looked up in alarm. A great eagle sat on her child, soothing it with its wings! The woman, afraid that the eagle would harm her baby, ran forward and the eagle flew away. Taking her child she returned to her village, somewhat shaken by the experience. The next day the same thing happened and when the woman returned home that night, she told her husband of the gentle eagle. He refused to believe that such a thing was possible. The next day, when the eagle came again, the woman

ran to get her husband to show him this wonder. The husband came but brought his bow and arrows and, alarmed for his child's safety, shot two arrows at the great bird. At that instant the eagle dodged and the arrows pierced the child, killing it instantly. The eagle was kind but the father had tried to kill it. The eagle cursed him, saying, "Now is kindness among men at an end, because you killed your child. Beginning with you, and going on to all people, you shall kill each other." To this day it is so.

CHANGING VIEWS

$\mathcal{I}$n our modern world, we have persecuted eagles in many ways, and our actions have been justified by "authoritative" descriptions of eagles and other raptors as being of dubious moral character, as in this quote from Thomas Bewick's *A History of British Birds* (1847):

THE CHARACTERS OF birds of the ravenous kind are particularly striking, and easily to be distinguished; the formidable talons, the large head, the strong and crooked beak, indicate their ability for rapine and carnage; their dispositions are fierce, and their nature is untractable; cruel and unsociable, they avoid the haunts of civilization, and retire to the most gloomy and wild recesses, where they can enjoy, in solitude, the fruits of their depredation.

The passing of forty-seven years brings more knowledge and a more favorable description, as in this quote from S. G. Goodrich and A. Winchell's *Johnson's Natural History* (1894):

STERN AND UNSOCIAL in their character, yet confident in their strength and efficient means of defense, the eagles delight to

WINTER FEEDING GROUNDS
Brought together by a localized abundance of food, these bald eagles co-exist in relative peace. At other times and in other locations, a single nesting pair of bald eagles might occupy and repel intruders from a territory measuring two square miles (5.2 km²) or more.
(Photo © Tom & Pat Leeson)

THE POWER OF EAGLE FEATHERS

At one time a party of Delawares were driven by the Pawnees to the summit of a high hill in their hunting-grounds. Here the chief warrior, driven almost to despair, sacrificed his horse to the tutelar spirit. Suddenly an eagle, rushing down from the sky, bore off the victim in his talons, and mounting into the air, dropped a feather from his wing. The chief caught it up with joy, and leading his followers down the hill, cut through the enemy without any one of his party receiving a wound.

—Rushton Dorman, *The Origin of Primitive Superstitions*, 1881

Eagle feathers are considered by many cultures to be incredibly powerful, valuable possessions. The Cheyenne people tell the following story to explain the history behind this belief. This version is based on one related by Kathleen Dugan in *The Vision Quest of the Plains Indians* (1985):

A Cheyenne man who lived long ago, before people had learned to use eagle feathers for ceremonial purposes, went on a vision quest. High into the mountains he climbed and, finding an appropriate spot, fasted and prayed for five days. He prayed that a powerful being would come to him and help him to find a cure for his troubles. He seemed to hear a voice telling him to be brave, no matter what he might see. Then seven eagles appeared, and one of them spoke to him. "Look at my feathers and see how they can be used to help you and your people." The eagle showed him how to make headdresses and ornaments from feathers and told the man that if his people used only eagle feathers, it would help them in war. Then the

eagles shook themselves and out fell feathers, which the man gathered and took home. His people made him a great leader for bringing them this gift.

Eagle feathers were important not only in war ceremonials and objects, but also in many healing rituals. They also played central roles in the eagle dance, and were used along with eagle-bone whistles in the sun dance. Several methods were used to obtain eagle feathers for ceremonial purposes. Some Central and South American peoples kept captive harpy eagles to supply them with feathers as they needed them. The Hopi people of the American Southwest sent special expeditions, directed by their religious leaders, to remove young golden eagles from the nest. The eaglets, after being carried to the village in cradleboards, then had their heads washed and were given presents. They were fed and taken care of until after the Niman ceremony, when they were "sent home" by being smothered. After the birds were skinned, prayer smoke was blown over their bodies. Then the corpses were sprinkled with cornmeal and buried in a special burial ground reserved for hawks and eagles.

Another method of gathering eagle feathers is described by George Laycock in *Autumn of the Eagle* (1973):

The Cheyenne brave killed the eagle for its feathers but did so only with strict attention to ancient ceremonial details, which included a formal apology to the spirit of the bird. The ritual was lengthy and demanding. The brave went into his lodge alone and through the long, dark night sang the sacred tribal chants reserved for the occasion. The following morning he emerged from his lodge to go into the plains and select the place for capturing the eagle, a place readily seen by the eagle in the sky. There he dug a hole in which to crouch and wait, but he dug with great care, working only when there were no eagles in sight, and carrying the earth away to avoid discovery of his plans by the sharp eyes of the eagle. Then he gathered long grass to lay over the pit as a roof.

On the day of the capture the warrior would bathe, then cover his body with oils to mask the man odor. Before the first yellow light of dawn he slipped off silently to crouch hidden in the pit beneath the brown grass. Above him, he placed a dead rabbit or other fresh bait, lashed down securely to prevent the eagle from swooping in and carrying it away.

At last the eagle would circle the blue morning sky, then come steadily and swiftly closer on its widespread wings. It would settle on the meat, begin tearing at it, and become so driven by its hunger that it would not see the brown hands reaching slowly up through the grass below it. Then the eagle would be dragged struggling and flapping down into the pit. There, according to Cheyenne custom, it could be killed in only one manner, by strangulation with a noose. Having taken eagles with his bare hands, the brave could walk with great pride among his people. He also gained a practical advantage, as the barter value of the feathers was high. Twenty eagle feathers might pay for a horse.

Today in the United States and Canada, eagle feathers may be obtained for ceremonial purposes only by special permit. Eagles and eagle parts from dead birds that have been found or confiscated are distributed through government agencies to the native peoples. They are then allotted by the elders of each group according to need. In 1994, the National Fish and Wildlife Forensics Laboratory in Ashland, Oregon, gave away 870 eagles and filled 28,000 requests for feathers.

BALD EAGLE AND EAGLET
Eagles are faithful parents, feeding, sheltering, and defending their chicks. In some of the large tropical forest eagle species, such as the harpy eagle, young eagles remain with their parents for up to a year after the time they make their first flight. (Photo © Henry H. Holdsworth)

WAR BONNET
A Native American war bonnet from the 1920s from the Fort Belknap Indian Reservation, Montana. The headdress is made of eagle feathers, eagle down, horse hair, beads, and ribbon. (Photo courtesy Buffalo Bill Historical Center, Cody, Wyoming)

dwell in the solitude of inaccessible rocks, on whose summits they build their rude nest and sit in lone majesty, while with their keen and piercing eye they sweep the plains below, even to the horizon. The combined extent and minuteness of their vision, often including not merely towns, villages and districts, but countries and even kingdoms in its vast circuit, at the same time carefully piercing the depths of forests, the mazes of swamps, and the intricacies of lawns and meadows, so as to discover every moving object—even the sly and stealthy animals that constitute their prey—form a power of sight to which human experience makes no approach. If we connect with this amazing gift of vision the power of flight which enables these birds to shoot through the heavens so as to pass from one zone to another in a single day and at a single flight, we shall readily comprehend how it is that they have in all ages so impressed the popular imagination as to render them the standing types and emblems of power.

More time passes and romanticism overwhelms science, as in this passage from Herbert Ravenal Sass's *On the Wings of a Bird* (1929):

THERE IS SOMETHING superb and glorious in the spectacle of the king of birds . . . manifesting his sovereignty, something that lifts the eagle above all other birds and invests him with an incomparable majesty. It is the majesty of perfectly proportioned beauty, of physical perfection in one of its most admirable forms.

By 1934, admiration of the eagle is coupled with defense of its existence, as in Frances Hobart Herrick's *The American Eagle* (1934):

THE EAGLE HAS come to possess a magic name, and its appeal has been felt by every great nation under the sun. The grandeur of its flight into the clouds, its preternatural keenness of vision, its very feathers even, have stirred the imagination of men in every age and clime from prehistoric times to the present day.

Strong, swift, majestic, making his playground in the clouds and defying the storm, no wonder the glamour of legend has crowned the eagle "King of Birds," the undisputed ruler of the sky, and made him the emblem of freedom, the incentive to valor, and the pledge of victory. But whether we regard the eagle as a legitimate king or only as a pirate chief who exacts unjust tribute from his more law-abiding subjects, every one must admit that the majesty of his appearance adds a touch of grandeur to the wild mountainside or rugged shore of lake or ocean which are his favorite abodes.

It's interesting to note the changing view of eagles, from rapacious killer to majestic ruler of the sky. The birds didn't change, but our moralistic interpretation of them did. For eagles, as with so many other animals, it's not any innate "evil" that leads to their persecution or any essential "good" that results in their glorification. In every era, the current image of an animal is that which is reflected in the mirror of the times, distorted by the limits of knowledge and warped by human self-interest. Whether that image is "good" or "bad" has far more to do with the observer than with the subject.

Today, our idea of what an eagle is comes from what we see on television, what we read in books, or, rarely, what we are able to observe firsthand. In creating their images of eagles, ancient peoples would seem to have had less information with which to work, but they didn't limit themselves strictly to their observations of the eagles flying above them. They added spiritual qualities to the eagles they saw and imagined fabulous birds who showed great "eagleness." The ancient legends tell us of the eagle's power; modern facts tell us of the eagle's plight. Neither gives us the complete picture of an eagle, but perhaps by considering both, we can appreciate the unique role these magnificent creatures play in our world. In "The Eagle" (1927), poet James Daly wrote:

If you would see him,
Wait on desolate crags
Where the near clouds are cold.
Wait, and over the third peak
At dawn you will see a greater
Than yourself.

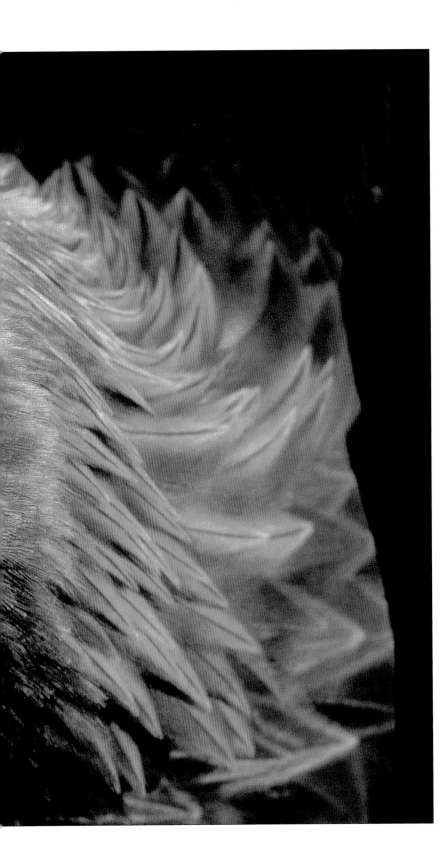

Your own
Remembered shadow, cast
On stone by a far moon
(All night your dark companion
And your comforter), will loom
Bleak in your mind under
The shadow of great wings reeling
And tumbling down the sky.

Tumbling and screaming down that bold
Steep sky, past you and past
Your shadow, down and down—

The mighty bird will dim
All wingless images in your eyes,
And drown all lesser cries
Your ears have known.

Eagles have captured the human imagination throughout our shared existence—an existence, for eagles, now under constant threat. Only respect for eagles will lead to action to ensure that eagles hold as prominent a place in the world of the future as they held in the world of the past. The alternative is unacceptable. Who among us wants to live beneath a sky in which eagles never soar?

GOLDEN EAGLE
Powerful symbol of the past, vulnerable inhabitant of the present—it is our actions, or lack of them, that will decide the eagle's future. (Photo © W. Perry Conway)

THE BEAKS OF EAGLES

An eagle's nest on the head of an old redwood on one of
    the precipice-footed ridges
Above Ventana Creek, that jagged country which
    nothing but a falling meteor will ever plow; no
    horseman
Will ever ride there, no hunter cross this ridge but the
    winged ones, no one will ever steal the eggs from
    this fortress.
The she-eagle is old, her mate was shot long ago, she is
    now mated with a son of hers.
When lightning blasted her nest she built it again on
    the same tree, in the splinters of the thunder-bolt.
The she-eagle is older than I; she was here when the fires
    of 'eighty-five raged on these ridges,
She was lately fledged and dared not hunt ahead of them
    but ate scorched meat. The world has changed in
    her time;
Humanity has multiplied, but not here; men's hopes and
    thoughts and customs have changed, their powers
    are enlarged,

Their powers and their follies have become fantastic,
The unstable animal never has been changed so rap-
    idly. The motor and the plane and the great war
    have gone over him,
And Lenin has lived and Jehovah died: while the
    mother-eagle
Hunts her same hills, crying the same beautiful and
    lonely cry and is never tired; dreams the same
    dreams,
And hears at night the rock-slides rattle and thunder in
    the throats of these living mountains.
                It is good for man
To try all changes, progress and corruptions, powers,
    peace and anguish, not to go down the dinosaur's
    way
Until all his capacities have been explored: and it is
    good for him
To know that his needs and nature are no more changed
    in fact in ten thousand years than the beaks of
    eagles.

                            —Robinson Jeffers

SOARING EAGLE
We are not the owners of the world around us, but merely the caretakers. We have been given the company of eagles, not as a gift but as a trust. Let us make certain that the privilege of watching a soaring eagle is one that future generations will have. (Photo © Frank Oberle)

Bibliography

Adams, Richard C. *Legends of the Delaware Indians and Picture Writing*. Washington, D.C.: 1905.

African Folktales and Sculptures. New York: Pantheon Books, 1952.

Allen, Thomas B. *Guardian of the Wild*. Bloomington: Indiana University Press, 1987.

Armstrong, Edward A. *The Life and Lore of the Bird: In Nature, Art, Myth, and Literature*. New York: Crown, 1975.

Audubon, John James. *The Birds of America*, vol. 1. New York: Dover Publications, 1967. Replication of work first published 1827–1838.

Bagley, Clarence B. *Indian Myths of the Northwest*. Seattle: Shorey Publications, 1982. First published by Lowman & Hanford, 1930.

Barbeau, Marius. *Haida Myths: Illustrated in Argillite Carvings*. National Museum of Canada, Department of Resources and Development Bulletin no. 127, Anthropological Series, no. 32, 1953.

Bent, Arthur Cleveland. *Life Histories of North American Birds of Prey*, Part 1. New York: Dover Publications, 1961. Originally published as Smithsonian Institution Bulletin 167, 1937.

Bewick, Thomas. *A History of British Birds, Volume 1: Containing the History and Description of Land Birds*. Newcastle, England: J. Blackwell & Co., 1847.

Blake, William. *The Writings of William Blake*, vol. 1. Edited by Geoffrey Keynes. London: Nonesuch Press, 1925.

Boswall, Jeffery. *Birds for All Seasons*. London: BBC Publications, 1986.

Brandon-Cox, H. *Summer of a Million Wings: Arctic Quest for the Sea Eagle*. New York: Taplinger Publishing, 1974.

Brazil, Mark. "Where Eastern Eagles Dare." *New Scientist*, (4 May 1991).

Brehm, Alfred Edmund. *From North Pole to Equator: Studies of Wild Life and Scenes in Many Lands*. London: Blackie & Son, 1896.

Broley, Myrtle Jeanne. *Eagle Man*. New York: Pellegrini & Cudahy, 1952.

Brown, Joseph Epes. *The Spiritual Legacy of the American Indian*. New York: Crossroad Publishing, 1982.

Brown, Leslie. *Eagles*. New York: Arco Publishing, 1970.

_____. *Eagles of the World*. Newton Abbot, England: David & Charles, 1976.

Brown, Leslie, and Dean Amadon. *Eagles, Hawks and Falcons of the World*, vols. 1 and 2. New York: McGraw-Hill, 1968.

Brown, Leslie H., Emil K. Urban, and Kenneth Newman. *The Birds of Africa*, vol. 1. London: Academic Press (Harcourt Brace Jovanovich), 1982.

Browning, Robert. *The Poetical Works of Robert Browning*. Edited by Ian Jack and Robert Inglesfield. Oxford: Clarendon Press, 1995.

_____. *The Works of Robert Browning*, vol. 10. London: Ernest Benn, 1912.

Brundage, Burr Cartwright. *The Fifth Sun: Aztec Gods, Aztec World*. Austin: University of Texas Press, 1979.

Burland, Cottie. *North American Indian Mythology*. Feltham, England: Hamlyn, 1985. First published by Newnes Books, 1965.

Burton, Philip. *Vanishing Eagles*. New York: Dodd, Mead, 1983.

Byron, Lord. *The Complete Poetical Works*. Edited by Jerome J. McGann. Oxford: Clarendon Press, 1980.

Caduto, Michael J., and Joseph Bruchac. *The Native Stories from Keepers of the Animals*. Golden, Colo.: Fulcrum, 1992; Saskatoon, Sask.: Fifth House Publishers, 1992.

Carson, Rachel. *Silent Spring*. Boston: Houghton Mifflin, 1962 and 1987.

Catlin, George. *Letters and Notes on the Manners, Customs, and Conditions of the North American Indians*, vols. 1 and 2. New York: Dover Publications, 1973. First published by D. Bogue, 1844.

Clare, John. "Shadows of Taste." In E. F. Linssen, *Nature Interlude: A Book of Natural History Quotations*. London: Williams and Norgate, 1951.

Collar, N. J, M. J. Crosby, and A. J. Stattersfield. *Birds to Watch 2: The World List of Threatened Birds*. Cambridge: Birdlife International, 1994.

Cooper, J. C. *Dictionary of Symbolic and Mythological Animals*. San Francisco: Thorsons, 1992.

Craig, Terry. "Will Eagles Always Soar?" Saskatoon *Star-Phoenix*, (27 December 1995).

Curtis, Edward S. *The North American Indian: Being a Series of Volumes Picturing and Describing the Indians of the United States and Alaska*, vols. 6 and 7. New York: Johnson Reprint Company, 1970. First published in 1911 by the author.

Cushing, Frank Hamilton. *Zuñi Folk Tales*. New York: Alfred A. Knopf, 1931.

Daly, James. "The Eagle." In "Three Poets." *The New Republic*, vol. 50. (6 April 1927).

deKay, Charles. *Bird Gods*. New York: A.S. Barnes, 1898.

del Hoyo, Josep, Andrew Elliott, and Jordi Sargatal et. Al. *Handbook of the Birds of the World*, vol. 2. Barcelona: Lynx Edicions, 1994.

Dennis, John V. "Rock-a-bye Birdie." *The Living Bird Quarterly*, Summer 1990.

Devoe, Alan. "Down to Earth." *American Mercury*, vol. 44, 1938.

Dorman, Rushton M. *The Origin of Primitive Superstitions and Their Development into the Worship of Spirits and the Doctrine of Spiritual Agency among the Aborigines of America.* Philadelphia: J.B. Lippincott, 1881.

Dugan, Kathleen Margaret. *The Vision Quest of the Plains Indians.* Lewiston, N.Y.: Edwin Mellen Press, 1985.

Dunlap, Thomas R. *Saving America's Wildlife.* Princeton: Princeton University Press, 1988.

"East German Police Keep Eagle Eye on Eggs." *New Scientist*, (4 August 1990).

Emerson, Ralph Waldo. *Collected Poems and Translations.* New York: The Library of America, 1994.

Frey, Rodney, editor. *Stories That Make the World: Oral Literature of the Indian Peoples of the Inland Northwest as told by Lawrence Aripa, Tom Yellowtail, and Other Elders.* Norman: University of Oklahoma Press, 1995.

Friar, Stephen, editor. *A Dictionary of Heraldry.* New York: Harmony Books, 1987.

Funk & Wagnalls Standard Dictionary of Folklore, Mythology, and Legend. New York: Funk & Wagnalls, 1972.

Gardiner, Linda. *Rare, Vanishing & Lost British Birds: Compiled from Notes by W. H. Hudson.* New York: E.P. Dutton, 1923.

Gargett, Valerie. *The Black Eagle: A Study.* Randburg, South Africa: Acorn Books and Russel Friedman Books, 1990.

Génsbøl, Benny. *Collins Guide to the Birds of Prey of Britain and Europe, North Africa and the Middle East.* London: Collins, 1984.

Gerrard, Jon M., and Gary R. Bortolotti. *The Bald Eagle: Haunts and Habits of a Wilderness Monarch.* Washington: Smithsonian Institution Press, 1988; Saskatoon, Sask.: Western Producer Prairie Books, 1988.

Gilbert, H. A., and Arthur Brook. *The Secrets of the Eagle: And of Other Rare Birds.* London: Arrowsmith, 1925.

Gill, Sam D., and Irene F. Sullivan. *Dictionary of Native American Mythology.* Denver: ABC-CLIO, 1992.

Goodrich, S. G., and A. Winchell. *Johnson's Natural History.* New York: Henry G. Allen, 1894.

Gordon, Seton. *The Golden Eagle: King of Birds.* London: Collins, 1955.

Graham, Frank, Jr. *The Audubon Ark: A History of the National Audubon Society.* New York: Alfred A. Knopf, 1990.

Graham, Frank, Jr. "Winged Victory." *Audubon*, July-August 1994.

"Gunning for Bald Eagles." *Newsweek*, (27 February 1989).

Hamerstrom, Frances. *An Eagle to the Sky.* Ames, Iowa: Iowa State University Press, 1970.

Herrick, Francis H. "Daily Life of the American Eagle: Early Phase." *The Auk*, vol. 49, 1932.

_____. "Daily Life of the American Eagle: Early Phase (concluded)." *The Auk*, vol. 50, 1933.

_____. *The American Eagle: A Study in Natural and Civil History.* New York: D. Appleton-Century, 1934.

Humphrey, P. W. "Eagle Lore." *Birds and Nature*, vol. 8, 1900.

Huxley, Julian. *African View.* London: Chatto & Windus, 1936.

Jeffers, Robinson. *The Collected Poetry of Robinson Jeffers*, vols. 1 and 2. Edited by Tim Hunt. Stanford: Stanford University Press, 1988.

Jobes, Gertrude. *Dictionary of Mythology Folklore and Symbols, Part 1.* New York: Scarecrow Press, 1962.

Jones, Thomas Rymer. *Cassell's Book of Birds*, vol. 2. London: Cassell, Petter, and Galpin, circa 1880s.

Keats, John. *The Poems of John Keats.* Edited by Miriam Allott. Harlow, England: Longman, 1986.

Lavine, Sigmund A. *Wonders of the Eagle World.* New York: Dodd, Mead & Co., 1974.

Laycock, George. *Autumn of the Eagle.* New York: Charles Scribner's Sons, 1973.

Larousse World Mythology. London: Paul Hamlyn, 1965.

Leeming, David Adams. *Encyclopedia of Creation Myths.* Santa Barbara: ABC-CLIO, 1994.

Legends of the Mighty Sioux. Compiled by Workers of the South Dakota Writers' Project, Work Projects Administration. Interior, S.Dak.: Badlands National History Association, 1987. First published by A. Whitman, 1941.

Line, Les. "Giants of the Eagle Kind." *International Wildlife*, July/August 1996.

Love, John A. *The Return of the Sea Eagle.* Cambridge: Cambridge University Press, 1983.

"Madagascar Serpent Eagle Rediscovered." *Newsletter of the World Working Group on Birds of Prey & Owls*, no. 19/20, 1994.

Markman, Roberta H., and Peter T. Markman. *The Flayed God: the Mesoamerican Mythological Tradition: Sacred Texts and Images from Pre-Columbian Mexico and Central America.* New York: HarperCollins, 1992.

Matthews, Washington. *Navaho Legends.* New York: Kraus Reprint Co., 1969. Originally published for the American Folklore Society by Houghton Mifflin, 1897.

Matthiessen, Peter. *Wildlife in America.* New York: Viking, 1959.

Mercatante, Anthony S. *Facts on File Encyclopedia of World Mythology and Legend.* New York: Facts On File, 1988.

Merkur, Daniel. *Powers Which We Do Not Know: the Gods and Spirits of the Inuit.* Moscow, Idaho: University of Idaho Press, 1991.

Meyburg, B.-U., and R. D. Chancellor, editors. *Raptors in the Modern World: Proceedings of the III World Conference on Birds of Prey and Owls.* Eilat, Israel, 22–27 March 1987. Berlin, London & Paris: World Working Group on Birds of Prey and Owls, 1989.

Miller, David G. Unpublished notes. Saskatoon, Sask.: 1987.

Miller, Mary, and Karl Taube. *The Gods and Symbols of Ancient Mexico and the Maya: An Illustrated Dictionary of Mesoamerican Religion*. London: Thames and Hudson, 1993.

Moody, Charles Stuart. "An Aërial Gymnast." *Bird Lore*, vol. 11, November-December 1909.

Mountfort, Guy. *Rare Birds of the World*. Lexington, Mass.: The Stephen Greene Press, 1988.

Murie, Olaus J. "A Price on His Golden Head." *Audubon Magazine*, vol. 54, July-August 1952.

Murphy, Robert. *The Golden Eagle*. New York: E.P. Dutton & Co., 1965.

Native American Myths and Legends. New York: SMITHMARK, 1994.

Newman, Edward. "The Eagles of Poetry and Prose." *The Zoologist*. November 1876.

Newton, Ian. *Population Ecology of Raptors*. Vermillion, S.Dak.: Buteo Books, 1979.

Olendorff, Richard R. *An Extensive Bibliography on Falconry, Eagles, Hawks, Falcons, and Other Diurnal Birds of Prey*. Fort Collins, Colo.: 1968–1970.

————. *Golden Eagle Country*. New York: Knopf, 1975.

Pack, Arthur Newton. "Blood Money for Eagles." *North American Review*, vol. 226, 1928.

Page, Jake, and Eugene S. Morton. *Lords of the Air: The Smithsonian Book of Birds*. Washington, D.C.: Smithsonian Books, 1989.

Percival, James. *The Poetical Works of James Gates Percival*. Boston: Ticknor and Fields, 1859.

Perry, Philip. *Birds of Prey*. Godalming, England: Colour Library Books, 1990.

Peyser, Marc. "Between a Wing and a Prayer." *Newsweek*, (19 September 1994).

Rasmussen, Knud. *The Eagle's Gift: Alaska Eskimo Tales*. Garden City, N.Y.: Doubleday, Doran & Company, 1932.

Redford, Polly. *Raccoons and Eagles: Two Views of American Wildlife*. New York: E.P. Dutton & Co., 1965.

Regenstein, Lewis. *The Politics of Extinction*. New York: Macmillan, 1975.

Roberts, Charles G.D. *The Lord of the Air*. Boston: Colonial Press, C.H. Simonds & Co., 1927. First published by L.C. Page & Co., 1904.

Rowland, Beryl. *Birds with Human Souls*. Knoxville: University of Tennessee Press, 1978.

Sass, Herbert Ravenal. *On the Wings of a Bird*. Garden City, N.Y.: Doubleday, Doran & Company, 1929.

Savage, Candace. *Eagles of North America*. Saskatoon, Sask.: Western Producer Prairie Books, 1987.

Schuon, Frithjof. *The Feathered Sun: Plains Indians in Art and Philosophy*. Bloomington, Ind.: World Wisdom Books, 1990.

Sibley, C. G., and B. L. Monroe. *Distribution and Taxonomy of Birds of the World*. New Haven, Conn.: Yale University Press, 1990.

Snyder, Noel F. R., and Helen A. Snyder. *Birds of Prey: Natural History and Conservation of North American Raptors*. Stillwater, Minn.: Voyageur Press, 1991.

Summers, Gerald. *Owned by an Eagle*. New York: E.P. Dutton, 1976.

Swainson, Charles. *Provincial Names and Folk Lore of British Birds*. London: Trübner and Co., 1885.

Teale, Edwin Way. "Bird of Freedom." *Atlantic Monthly*, vol. 200, 1957.

Tennyson, Alfred, Baron. *The Poetical Works of Tennyson*. Boston: Houghton Mifflin, 1974.

Thomson, James. *Poetical Works*. Edited by J. Logie Robertson. London: Oxford University Press, 1965.

Truslow, Frederick Kent. "Eye to Eye with Eagles." *National Geographic*, January 1961.

Tuchman, Gail. *Through the Eye of the Feather: Native American Visions*. Layton, Utah: Gibbs Smith, 1994.

Turbak, Gary. "America's Other Eagle." *National Wildlife*, October/November 1989.

Tyler, Hamilton A. *Pueblo Birds and Myths*. Norman: University of Oklahoma Press, 1991. Originally published in Civilization of the American Indian Series, vol. 147, University of Oklahoma Press, 1979.

Vanishing Species. New York: Time-Life, 1974.

Walker Art Center and The Minneapolis Institute of Arts. *American Indian Art: Form and Tradition*. New York: E.P. Dutton, 1972.

Wallace, Ernest, and E. Adamson Hoebel. *The Comanches: Lords of the South Plains*. Norman: University of Oklahoma Press, 1952.

Walters, Anna Lee. *The Spirit of Native America: Beauty and Mysticism in American Indian Art*. Vancouver: Raincoast Books, 1989.

Watson, J., A. F. Leitch, and R. A. Broad. "The Diet of the Sea Eagle *Haliaeetus albicilla* and Golden Eagle *Aquila chrysaetos* in Western Scotland." *Ibis*, vol. 134, 1992.

Wetmore, Alexander. "The Eagle, King of Birds, and His Kin." *National Geographic*, July 1933.

"White-tailed Sea Eagle Makes a Comeback in Greenland." *Newsletter of the World Working Group on Birds of Prey & Owls*, no. 12, June 1990.

Willis, Roy. *Signifying Animals: Human Meaning in the Natural World*. London: Unwin Human, 1990.

Wilson, Alexander, and Charles Lucian Bonaparte. *American Ornithology or the Natural History of the Birds of the United States*, vol. 1. Philadelphia: Porter & Coates, 1898. Reprint of work originally published 1808–1814.

Acknowledgments

Thanks to Tom Lebovsky for the opportunity to write this book, to Michael Dregni for his valuable insights and encouragement, to Todd Berger for photo acquisitions, and to everyone at Voyageur Press for their commitment to making this project extremely enjoyable. Thank you to Jane Billinghurst for her editing skills, and to David and Cathryn Miller for their invaluable proofreading and comments. Additional thanks to David and to Dr. Stuart Houston for including me on several forever-to-be-remembered banding trips, and to Dr. Houston for his thorough reading of the manuscript. Any errors remaining in the text are mine. Also, thank you to Dr. Gary Bortolotti for his kind assistance despite a hectic schedule.

A big thank you to my family for their constant encouragement, with special thanks to my sister, Jane, who is simply wonderful. To my husband, Glen, who patiently and cheerfully read what was placed before him, I give the award for best (and briefest) constructive criticisms. And finally, to my elderly rabbit, Freddy, who passed away as this work neared completion, I send my gratitude for long hours of companionship as I researched and wrote—bon voyage, little friend.

Organizations to Contact to Help Endangered Eagles

Birdlife International
Wellbrook Court
Girton Road
Cambridge CB3 0NA
U.K.

The Philippine Eagle Foundation
No. 1 North Street
DBP Village
Matina, Davao City 8000
Philippines

National Audubon Society
950 Third Avenue
New York, NY 10022

World Wildlife Fund
1250 24th Street NW
Washington, DC 20037-1175

World Wildlife Fund
90 Eglinton Avenue East, Suite 504
Toronto, ON M4P 2Z7
Canada

Index